LESSONS LEARNED

FIND YOURSELF

DATING A NARCISSIST

MARIA MARIA BINDER

FIND YOURSELF

Maria Maria Binder

This book reflects the author's present recollections of experiences over time. All names and characteristics have been changed, some events have been compressed, and some dialogue has been recreated.

No identification with actual persons (living or deceased), places, buildings, and products should be inferred.

Author photo: Rob MacDonald, Revolutions Per Minute Media

Editor: Winnie O'Brien

Join me on social media:

Instagram: @bememorablemindfulmotivated

LinkedIn:
https://www.linkedin.com/company/bememorablemindfulmotivated/

Facebook:
https://www.facebook.com/BeMemorableMindfulMotivated

Website: www.be-memorable.com

ISBN: 978-1-7388126-1-5 Electronic book

ISBN: 978-1-7388126-0-8 Book

DEDICATION

"Find Yourself" is dedicated to all those
that find strength in themselves.

Those who follow their heads, hearts, and intuition.

For those who love fiercely and want the best
for themselves and others.

Keep this world loving and full of gratitude.

Be Memorable, Mindful & Motivated!

In loving memory of my mom, Maria Binder

CONTENTS

ACKNOWLEDGMENTS

This book has been a labour of love and provided so much healing to my heart and mind. But none of this happens without love and support; I had so much of it while writing this book.

I want to thank my best friend, Annie Paterson, for supporting me throughout these years. She had an open heart, so much empathy, and sound advice on how to move forward. Her love and support carried me daily and made me a better person.

Julia Rooney, my non-bio sister, helps me believe in myself like no other. This project and my vision are championed and supported wholeheartedly; without her, my dream of authoring this book would still be on my computer. Her tireless coaching and support kept me accountable and is so very much appreciated.

Winnie O'Brien and I sat in a room not so long ago when I was exhausted trying to finalize this book, and our conversation breathed new life into me. We promised each other we would support each other's dreams, and when we finished our conversation and promises, we felt like we were going to blow the roof off the building we were in. Winnie helped me believe in this project and stepped in when I so desperately needed it.

Friends are an essential part of your life, journey, and purpose. They hold you accountable for your actions, show empathy when needed, and hold your hand through the most challenging moments. With this, I acknowledge the people mentioned above again and add my great allies, Barb Long, Maia Kapach, Dewi Wood, Joy Tamke, Rob MacDonald, and Kim Caputo, for believing in me and my dreams.

Prologue

"Find Yourself" helps readers to recognize the signs of narcissism. Based on real-life scenarios, we explore signs and ask ourselves thought provoking questions about our relationships. Through engagement and sharing experiences, we find ourselves and regain our power.

This book is based on real-life experiences. Victims recount the type of emotional, relationship-based abuse many of us are familiar with. Most willingly stay in these relationships until they can no longer preserve their self, their dignity or their sanity. People in these scenarios continually doubt their thoughts, decisions, and self-worth, until they can no longer tolerate being gaslit by their partners —all traits of narcissistic abuse and the ensuing personal journeys.

Gaslighting, as explained, is a form of emotional abuse that is seen in abusive relationships. It is the act of manipulating a person by forcing them to question their thoughts, memories, and the events occurring around them. Gaslighting victims can be pushed so far that they question their sanity.

In sharing this book, we wanted to share the journey as it is not as easy as it would appear to walk away from this type of relationship. It took years of finding ourselves through therapy, self-reflection and a healthy amount of tears to recover from this situation.

We share our story with you and ask insightful questions to help you recognize your worth and to support you in identifying your own situation.

Everyone is on their own journey, but we can learn from one another. Let us share and learn together.

Before you start this book let us recognize some characteristics of a narcissist.

Gaslighting is a form of emotional abuse that results from the act of manipulating a person by coercing them to question their thoughts, memories, and the events occurring around them. Gaslighting victims can be pushed to the brink of questioning their own sanity (Stark, 2019).

Some individuals struggle with narcissistic tendencies and these personality challenges can present an inflated sense of self, an excessive requirement for admiration, and a lack of empathy for others. This can cultivate turmoil in relationships and a false sense of confidence. Behind this mask of extreme confidence lies a fragile sense of self that is vulnerable to the slightest assessment.

An individual with narcissistic tendencies may experience complications throughout many areas of life, such as financial endeavours, relationships, careers, and academia. The result of these complications may include general dissatisfaction in life or disappointment when they do not experience the admiration they expect and believe they deserve.

While indications may vary, according to Mayo Clinic's, signs and symptoms of narcissistic tendencies, individuals with this trait can:

- Have an increased sense of self-importance
- Have an exaggerated sense of entitlement
- Expect to be recognized despite efforts that warrant their achievements
- Exaggerate achievements and aptitudes
- Be preoccupied with fantasies about power and success
- Dominate conversations and belittle individuals they perceive as inferior
- Expect special favours and compliance
- Take advantage of other's emotions
- Reduced empathy
- Behave arrogantly or boastful

- Insist on having the best, even if possessions or credentials are outside of their means

Simultaneously, individuals with narcissistic tendencies experience criticism in a harsh manner and can:

- Become impatient or angry
- Have significant problems with interpersonal communication
- Have difficulty with self-regulation
- Experience major problems in a stressful environment
- Experience perfectionistic tendencies
- Have classified feelings of insecurity and shame

Recent clinical studies using empirical research have provided some insight into individuals with narcissistic traits. Empirical research is evidence-based studies founded on observations and measurements of phenomena, experienced first-hand by the researcher. Ultimately, recognizing the complex theory between individuals who display narcissistic behaviour and empathetic aptitude allows clinicians to better understand their structures of motivation. Research explains that individuals who display reduced empathy also display dysfunctional behavioural motivation (Baskin-Sommers et al., 2014). Narcissistic traits have a severe impact on close relatives, and should you personally require support, it is beneficial to seek assistance to help you navigate the impact that this behaviour has on others. According to Day, (2021) fluctuations between feeling like you are the most important person to feeling dismissed and gaslit are telltale signs that you are experiencing narcissism. Often struggling with feelings of abandonment and trauma themselves, when provoked, the individual struggling with these traits can further engage in jealous behaviour and abuse themselves (Kjærvik, & Bushman, 2021).

I JUST MET YOUR NEW EX-HUSBAND

My name is Myriah, and in 2005 I was employed as a sales representative selling surveillance systems. I worked independently for the most part, so teaming up with like-minded people was important. I arranged a group of people who sell items that complement what I do, to exchange leads and refer new business prospects. Tracy sold payroll services to new businesses, Tom sold merchant services, and Joe promoted a line of office supplies. Not only did we exchange business cards, but we also referred to each other's services. We always met in coffee shops and spent a lot of time 'bitching' about everything from sales to operations to service departments, including our clients. A necessary practice when in sales.

Tracy called me one morning, almost breathless, and said, "Myriah, I just met your new ex-husband." Having been married a few times already, I had mixed emotions about this statement but was intrigued, nonetheless. Greedily, I wanted the number to this new ex-husband. Tracy described this new prospect as tall, handsome, funny, and charming. I like all those things and needed more business, so it seemed like a win-win. I took the details and called immediately. Luckily, my new ex-husband instantly picked up the phone. I introduced myself and let him know how I obtained his number. I left out the ex-part, naturally, and he agreed to see me the next day. That seemed easy. Now, what to wear? Since I worked from home, I could spend all day prospecting, I mean, searching for the perfect outfit for my big meeting.

It was a Thursday morning, and I was enroute for my 9:00 am meeting at a commercial building. My new ex-husband, Luke, was starting an appliance manufacturing company that specialized in ice machines and ice storage bins and had just leased a new commercial property. The building was huge! As I pulled into the parking lot, I started to have some doubts; honestly, did I know that much about surveillance and how to secure a building this size? But, as we do, we 'fake it until we make it'. I called my new ex-husband to let him know I had arrived, and he came down from his office to let me in the front door. Tracy was right. He was tall and handsome for sure! He led me upstairs to his office - he had a desk, his cell phone, and a boyish grin that made me melt. This was going to be interesting!

Luke took me on a tour of his facility. So much space, so many doors – I had no clue what I was doing. Diligently, I took notes, scribbled schematics, and tried my best to seem knowledgeable about all that is surveillance. Ha! I thought to myself. This job is going to be a challenge.

I could barely breathe, trying to keep up with the tour while looking cute but professional. Once the tour was over, we headed back to Luke's office and started to chat about his new business and how things were progressing. Luke informed me he had secured a large deposit from a vendor looking for some equipment to be built. He had a credit card and a dream to start this company. I was impressed. But his sexual innuendo intrigued me more. Witty, clever, and cocky, just the way I wanted my new ex-husband. As we were chatting, I bluntly asked if Luke was married. He told me he had three kids. I assumed he was not married as he avoided that question, and just like that, it satisfied my need to know if he had a wife. He did not. Or did he? No matter, I let Luke know that I would take my highly detailed schematics and information back to the office and somehow provide a quote despite my limited knowledge on estimating this job. I went to leave. We shook hands as professionals do, and there it was. I still cannot describe it. It was like electric shocks going straight to my bathing suit area, and it rocked me. In addition to our friendly banter, easy conversation, and chemistry, I was convinced this was the beginning of what would prove to be a tumultuous relationship. I had no idea what I was in for, but I was in. I was determined, focused, and with my eye on the prize. I was going to land a deal and then land the deal, if you know what I mean.

And so, it began!

Ask Yourself and Meaningful Journaling

This section is meant to reflect on your own story and thoughtfully reflect on your relationships.

____

____

____

Have you ever ignored your intuition?

____

____

____

If yes, why didn't you listen to your intuition?

____

____

____

Do you think your intuition is always right?

____

____

____

How does one do a better job of trusting one's instinct?

____

____

____

GETTING DOWN TO BUSINESS

Although I am ambitious, I am a procrastinator. After meeting with Luke, I felt accomplished and appreciated the opportunity to manage this large deal. I also welcomed any chance to daydream about this handsome entrepreneur. However, I did procrastinate about completing my quote.

Like all things in my life, I have faith in the universe to help me in times of uncertainty. I did not know how to finalize this quote because my schematics looked like a child's drawing. I sat on it for a day and a half looking to the universe for some magical help, and then sheepishly took it to one of our service technicians to get the input I needed.

I had a very disgruntled hottie impatiently waiting for his quote by the time I was finally able to deliver. I perhaps made up a slight fib that my computer was out of commission, which he did not buy for a moment. He called me out on my inability to quote promptly and questioned my professionalism. It seemed overly harsh and blunt when his building had nothing to protect as of yet, and now that I look back, his angry reaction was a preview of what was to come. Because I was still reveling in the thought of that electric handshake that rocked me, I was willing to listen to any criticism he dished out. Somehow, I felt like I deserved that harsh tone in his voice.

Finally, I was able to get out the quote that would change my life, not only for the commission paid but the road to events to come that would impact my life forever. It is surprising to me now how much I pushed myself to get to know a narcissist, which at the time I had no knowledge of what this term or disorder even meant.

But more on that later.

Luke called me to review the contract in person, which excited me to no end. Not only was I excited, but I was also scared shitless too. I was afraid because I was presenting a large contract and making a big deal about seeing my gregarious new client again.

I am happy to say the meeting went well. Luke was satisfied with the quote as most of his business needs were met. Can I say I wanted to satisfy a few of my needs with this gorgeous man? I was pleasantly surprised he did not scold me for the lateness of getting the quote to him and only wanted to negotiate on the pricing which was in my control. So, the next step was to get the system installed. I set up an installation date based on my company's service protocols, which he immediately called me out on. I was learning that this man could not take anything at face value. He questioned everything and wanted the process to be modified for his needs regardless of my company's rules and standards. For some reason, I confused this frankly rude behaviour for business acumen and not for what it was - egocentric, unrealistic demands from a client. It was puzzling, but I was ridiculously drawn to this man and wanted to please him. In more ways than one.

The day before installing the hottie's surveillance system, I walked into our service department and confirmed the technicians would be there at the predetermined time. I wanted to ensure nothing would go wrong because a good salesperson shows up at 7:00 am to stickhandle the deal. To be honest, it was the only time I did this. But it seemed like a promising idea, as I couldn't wait to get in front of this handsome devil again.

With donuts in hand, I entered the facility again and cheerfully greeted an ever-so-happy-to-see-me business owner. The banter again started from the minute I walked through the door. The conversation came easily and the innuendo even more so. Since innuendo comes naturally to me, it truly is one of my favourite languages. And I was speaking HIS language too, it seemed he understood me completely. He made me feel like the most desired person when I was around him.

We went into his office, where we munched on donuts and waited for my technicians' call. As 7:00 am came and went, and while Luke sipped his daily Red Bull, which he drank instead of coffee, we waited and chatted some more. Thankfully, conversation was interesting because the techs still weren't there by 8:00 am, a time which came faster than I wanted to "cum" in my fantasy with this feisty new friend. I finally decided to excuse myself from the office to call my service department to get an updated estimated arrival time. My heart dropped when I found out one of the technicians had booked a doctor's appointment and had to reschedule. I was shocked and angry that no one from my office thought to update me. I thought somehow the universe was cock-blocking my opportunity to forge a relationship with the Red Bull-drinking man of my now dreams.

Was Luke annoyed to hear the news? You can bet your bottom dollar. Mad enough to think that somehow this was my fault? Yes again! You can imagine my embarrassment, but secretly I rejoiced, knowing I could make another appointment for the installation. And you know I would be there again, no question! I rescheduled for the following day and again made myself available to be on location, noting that this is what all salespeople did. I let him know how much I appreciated his understanding of this "mix" up.

Thankfully, my technicians showed up the following day. As you can guess, I was there at 7:00 am with a Red Bull and sweets in hand to greet the man with a vicious but sexy grin. Once the work commenced, I could easily sit back and make all the small chat in the world. We talked about everything, mainly about Luke, as he loved to talk about himself. As it turned out, he was a certified mechanic turned salesperson, turned entrepreneur. One could not help but be impressed with this man who developed a business that, in a few short years, would employ over 400 people and pump out millions of dollars in appliance manufacturing equipment. Successful enough to want this ambitious creature in my pants!

As the morning progressed, I was smart enough not to overstay my welcome. But before I left, I wanted to learn more about Luke's kids and the Mrs. Ex-Husband.

Luke was so happy to share stories of all his lovely offspring and one could quickly tell how much he loved his sons. Again, no mention of a 'Mrs.' - was he widowed, divorced, or separated? I left feeling bewildered but so intrigued. He walked me to the front door, and we said our goodbyes.

He shook my hand again and thanked me for the visit. When he grabbed and held my hand, which seemed like an eternity, I felt warmth from the bottom of my toes to my now hardened nipples. I felt flush and thought I was going to pass out. I was happy, curious, and excited and could not wait to call Tracy to tell her every detail. With that, I wondered if I would see him again now that the installation was done. A girl can dream!

Ask Yourself and Meaningful Journaling

This section is meant to reflect on your own story and thoughtfully reflect on your relationships.

____

____

____

Have you ever felt like a line of questioning was harsher than it should be?

____

____

____

Have you ever justified someone speaking harshly to you by thinking you deserved it or that you were at fault?

____

____

____

Have you been questioned at some time in your life why you allowed someone to treat you a certain way?

____

____

____

IF YOU WERE MY BOYFRIEND

It was time to follow up with my dreamboat. After every sale, it is essential to ensure that the client is happy with their equipment and service. And I wanted to service this client.

I strategically waited for midday to give this exciting creature a call. "Oh, hi, it's Myriah. Just calling to see if your surveillance system is working and if you are happy so far." My heart was beating out of my chest, I was so excited. "Yup, all is well. However, we seem to be having a slight issue with one of the cameras," Luke replied. I cannot remember when I was happier hearing that a client had an issue and that I might have to go back to check and rectify it. I told Luke I would schedule someone to look after that immediately. I wanted to keep the conversation going, so I asked how things were developing. He was excited to share that he was building offices and getting ready to hire staff. Okay, Myriah, make a move, ask him if he would like to go out for a drink. I typically am not that bold, but I felt compelled to see him. I cannot explain why I was so drawn to this entrepreneurial god. Luke responded with, "I'm super busy right now, so I can't commit to a time, but yes, we should at some time". It was not a no or a definite yes, but I was sure he would reach out and set up a time to meet.

This guy must have been busy because I hadn’t heard from my new heartthrob until two days later. I was convinced there was a connection. One could not possibly feel this way without the other not feeling the same. It's impossible. And then it happened, my phone rang. The call display finally gave me the sign for which I was waiting. I swear the phone display read, "I want you, Myriah!”.

Do not pick up on the first ring, you will seem desperate, goes the old dating mantra. Ha! It was because I felt so hypnotized by this man. I let my phone ring twice and then casually picked up and said, "Myriah speaking”, as if I did not know who it was and had not been waiting two days for this to happen. Mr. Red Bull A Day asked me how my day was going, and I was ecstatic that it didn't seem like an official work call. We chatted easily, and I felt so connected to him. We had talked for at least 45 minutes when I suggested again, we go out for a beer. I still didn't get a clear answer, so I replied with "three strikes and you're out", and I wasn't asking again. Who am I? Why was I this forward? With that, to my amazement, a date was made. He agreed to meet me for a beer at the local pub the next day. What was happening? This girl finally got her date! I worked hard for this but wondered why he was playing so hard to get.

He seemed so footloose and fancy-free but always so busy and occupied. I assumed this was because he was starting his new business and had a lot on his plate. It could not be because he had a wife. He never mentioned that he had one and didn't wear a ring. Did I need to dig deep to find out?

I woke up excited. Today is beer date day with my mysterious man. I putzed through my day and was counting down the hours. We were going to meet at 3:30 pm. I texted Luke at 2:30 pm to ensure we were still meeting and just an excuse to connect. He confirmed the time and told me he could not stay too long but would meet me there. I rolled into the pub where we agreed to meet and found a table on the patio. It was a warm afternoon, perfect to get this romance started. I ordered a pint of beer and waited for my handsome man to arrive. I saw him drive into the parking lot. I was delighted but started sweating with anticipation while trying to appear nonchalant.

As Luke walked up to the table, I could not stop staring at him. He was playful, light-hearted, seemed confident, and had some swagger. He sat down, ordered a beer, and the banter began. I felt intoxicated. I was drunk with desire. The conversation was easy; the innuendo filled me with passion, and I did not know what would unfold. I can still remember how tasty and delicious the beer was to this day. Perhaps I was drinking too fast or caught up in the tornado I secretly called "My Luke." I excused myself from the table to go to the lady's room. I strolled around his chair, touched his shoulder, and bent down to whisper in his ear. "If you were my boyfriend, I would let you have anal with me." Who am I? Why did I say that? I entered the washroom, went directly to the mirror, and looked at myself. What did I just say? It's not like I had a fondness for that particular act. So why in the hell would I even say that. I was mortified! How has this man taken hold of me so hard that I didn't even recognize my pushy, determined, and filthy manner? What was happening to me? I didn't care. I was so into this guy. I washed my hands, looked at myself, and thought 'let the games begin'.

I sat back at our table, slightly embarrassed but embracing the insanity. I was disappointed when my beer date said he had to leave early. Could it be because I scared him off with my anal comment? Why did it seem like he was always preoccupied, non-committal, and on the run? There was no reason given for the swift getaway that he had prepared me for, but perhaps it was what he wasn't saying. Luke asked for the bill and generously paid it. Somehow his urgent need to leave turned into us walking hand in hand down a short street that led into a river walk. We walked quickly together, and I was going crazy. Every nerve in my body was fired up. I wanted to be in this moment forever. In my newly deranged mind, I was floating on air and was soaking up every delicious moment. We decided to sit on the grass by the river. Hands locked into one another, and then it happened. I can't remember who instigated that kiss, but I wanted it so badly. I didn't anticipate this happening so quickly, but this girl had no complaints.

‘My Luke” now really had to go. I felt super special because he was in a hurry, but he had extended his time with me. At that moment, it didn't occur to me that he was going home for dinner and running late.

Nonetheless, my passionately irrational heart was flattered. I was in dreamland and confused about how I was acting and feeling, but I could not get enough.

Ask Yourself and Meaningful Journaling

This section is meant to reflect on your own story and thoughtfully reflect on your relationships.

____

____

____

Is it possible to go momentarily insane and act entirely not like yourself (I ask partly in jest, but that's how I felt)?

____

Have you ever been in that situation? Explain.

Have you ever felt subservient to someone?

Have you left your morals at the door and done something out of character for you?

___

___

___

ALIBIS, KNEE PADS, AND LATE-NIGHT RENDEZVOUS

The emotional texting affair begins, and I am delighted, except that it only seems to occur in the daytime. I'm told after-hours activities are reserved for his kids, and I understand. Well, of course, I do; I'm an adult and sensitive to children's needs.

I enjoyed an early morning text that was sent before I even woke. It feels delightful to know that I am the first person someone thinks of upon rising. Luke often reminded me of this 'thoughtfulness'. I take that and lie to myself about this new friendship. I wait for every text message that fills me with the hope that love might be around the corner for me.

I live my life for the next few weeks with my daytime chat partner and enjoy my sassy single-girl lifestyle in the evening hours. Not the worst scenario; however, every time my phone chirps with a new text message, my heart skips a beat, hoping it is from my daytime texting babe. Life is good, and I am enjoying everything that it brings me.

One afternoon, I got a text message asking if I would like to meet up for a beer with Luke and his best friend, Derek. Say what? Is text man asking me to meet his best friend for the dinner hour? This must be a good sign that things are going in the right direction. There could not possibly be a wife when I'm meeting his best friend. I am genuinely excited and automatically say I will join them. I get snazzy, and off I go to meet my new best friend and his best friend.

Luke is waiting for me at the table when I get to the bar. I greet him with a hug and a kiss on the cheek, so excited about this meet and greet. We order and enjoy our first sips of tasty beer and I learn that Derek and Luke have been friends for an exceedingly long time. Derek is single, and I sensed he might have a boy crush on Luke. They grew up in a small town where they pulled boyish pranks, then moved to Denver as adults. I honestly could not have cared less about meeting Derek as I was so smitten with the tasty treat in front of me. He was starting to steal my heart, and he knew it.

About half an hour into our date, in walks Derek, a happy bounce in his step and a cheerful little man from the looks of it. He seemed pleased to see his best buddy as they greeted one another. Luke introduced him to me, and we ordered more beers. I listened to funny antics from days of old and the shenanigans these two besties got up to; they seemed like two peas in a pod. I used to think you can tell a lot about people by the friends they choose. We shall learn more about that as the story unfolds.

In my mind, my relationship is getting further along. This is our second date - I'm meeting his best pal, and we are all having a few laughs and enjoying each other's company. Not for a moment did I think there might be an ulterior motive for Derek joining us, say that Luke might need an alibi to be out after the dinner hour for a drink. Derek sees the connection between

Luke and me, and we all carry on like we've known each other for years. Such a pleasant time. It was eventually getting late, so we all decided to head home. Luke walked me to my car and kissed me goodbye. After that kiss, I felt like I was now drowning in my underpants, just wanting more from this situation. Much more!

I woke up the following day swooning in the memory of the night before. I carry on with my day and get invited to have a few drinks with my besties. I love girl time with my friends. A time for wine, work chat, and our dogs. We all have dogs, and we enjoy getting together weekly. I have not yet told them about my little secret Luke. I'm not sure why I hadn't yet confided in them, but I was enjoying this journey and was not ready to share yet. Perhaps I would feel judged?

While wrapping up with these lovely ladies, I got a text from my new love. He was working at his shop and wondered if I'd like to come for a visit? Would I, indeed, I did!

I showered and readied myself for who knows what. I was so excited to see Luke in his work environment again and spend some alone time with him. It was about midnight when I arrived, and like clockwork, Luke was waiting for me at the front door to let me in. He was dressed in jeans, knee pads, and a t-shirt. I love a man that does manual labour. He was sectioning off an open space work area on the second floor of his office building. The space in front of his office will house his assistant and managers. In my fantasy, I am his apprentice and help him build his legacy and our future together from scratch. But for now, we shall sip on a few cocktails, talk about his dreams, and I will be his sidekick showing up in the middle of the night as his playdate. How did I not see any of these red flags? Only seeing him off hours, with a friend, texting only during the day. I was blinded by the feeling, like I was super special.

It was getting late, and we were still sitting around and chatting. Luke's tentative way with me was making me crazy for him. I felt at the time his lack of action was him respecting me and being a gentleman. As I reflect years later, because he wasn't truthful with me, I assumed he was waiting for me to make all the moves I was making. We started kissing in his boardroom, and it was fiery and hot. Kissing is so important and is the gateway to everything passionate. We kissed for what felt like hours. I couldn't take it anymore. I wanted to take it to the next level. Again, who is this girl?

I took some liberty and unbuckled his jeans, as I could barely wait for his pants to be off. I told him to sit down on the chair. I ripped off his knee pads and put them on myself. I kneeled in front of him and explored all that is Luke and his sexuality. I was so into this guy; it was easy for my mouth to make love to his cock. I wanted all of it. I wanted to please him so much. I took my time and flirted with just the tip of his cock. He was ready for me to take all of his gorgeous manhood into my mouth and throat, so I devoured his member to the best of my ability. Although I felt inferior to Luke most of the time for whatever reason, right now I was in control. While I was showing him who was the boss with his cock pulsating in my mouth, I steadily brought him to the brink and enjoyed all of his goodness as he released himself to me. I felt powerful at that moment, and so pleased with my performance. I cleaned up, finished my drink, and called it a night.

Ask Yourself and Meaningful Journaling

This section is meant to reflect on your own story and thoughtfully reflect on your relationships.

____

____

____

Is omitting the truth a lie?

____

____

____

Have you ever told yourself you were not actually lying by not telling the truth?

____

____

____

Why do we accept not being mutually respected in some relationships?

____

____

____

Does sex sometimes make you feel powerful?

____

____

____

INCH BY INCH

I guess I would get it any which way I could. Our rendezvous were getting more frequent and more intense. It felt like we were genuinely sneaking around, and I wasn’t sure what was being protected. I was so far into this situation, and my feelings were genuinely out of control. I felt connected but purposefully oblivious to what was happening in Mr. Mystery's life. I didn't want to be the catalyst for a broken relationship, but I was also convinced that I didn't want to know the truth. I wasn't sure I would get the entire truth even if I asked. But this was rolling faster than a high-speed train, and there was no stopping.

Calls and texts were ever so frequent, and my heart was wrapped up in Mr. Gregarious. Everything seemed so right but so wrong at the same time. My new squeeze had an answer for everything, and everything, I was told, was on the up and up.

My gentlemen caller set an early morning date to come to my house for the first time. An early morning 5:30

am visit. He wanted to visit before he went to work. Did that seem reasonable? I guess it was normal conduct when I had only two things on my mind. One was to see Luke anytime his schedule allowed, which was always on his timeline, and two, I wanted to have this man inside of me.

I set an alarm for 5:00 am to shower and look my best, all under the guise that he would just come in for a visit as I awoke.

Hoping that nothing would get between Mr. Luke and me before he got in between my sheets, was the only thing I worried about that morning. True to his (likely only) word, there was a subtle knock on the door right at 5:30 am.

I opened the door and led him directly to my bedroom. We talked and snuggled in my little double bed. I was so happy to have him in my home. Luke was delighted upon meeting my dog for the first time, which is an excellent telltale sign of a good man. Is it not? I seemed to be constantly trying to justify being with this man because intuitively I was convinced that everything wasn't as I was told or as it appeared.

I am a woman, and I had needs, and I wanted them fulfilled.
Work clothes seemed to be overrated at this time of the morning, so I asked Luke to undress and cuddle just a little closer. His skin was so electric to me. Everything just came naturally. New lovers are often awkward, but not in this case. Our bodies moved together like we had done this before. It was slow and deliberate. I was so into him and wanted him to take me and fuck me as hard as he could, but still felt this tentativeness about the situation. What could it be? Stupidly, I was making excuses, thinking we just wanted this to be meaningful and wonderful. Again, I was going to have to take control of this situation. I climbed on top of him and slowly started to grind on him.

I wanted to feel his hard cock against me. I wanted to ensure I was ready for this ever-so-exciting first time he was inside me. I enjoyed this man so intensely I ached for him. I ripped off my panties and started a slow and beautiful entry into my vagina. Inch by inch I received him, and it was so delightful. We kissed on the mouth harder and faster, with every thrust of his cock exploring every inch of my insides. It felt so good, so right being close to him. He came inside me, and it felt like I was going to heaven. This was the first of many visits to my place. Luke could come and go as he pleased, literally. Rarely did I get a visit after work hours, but early morning visits were always welcomed.

Something was up, and it wasn't always Luke's cock inside me. I felt like I was the other woman for some reason. It is not the best feeling, and I needed to figure out what would happen if we continued this sordid affair. My instincts grew louder and louder, and I needed to know the truth. At this point, however, the facts probably would not have changed anything because Luke made me feel like the most important person when we were together. It wasn't long before the "L" word was used. I fell in love with him quickly, but it was time to know exactly what I was dealing with.

Why was I so afraid to know the truth? I deserved to know, but I was scared that everything would change.

If there was actual infidelity, Luke realized admitting the ugly truth could have ended our love affair. I did not want that, but I also felt that this conversation was needed.

Luke always seemed annoyed when I brought up the subject, like I was the one doing something wrong. I was wrong in not pressing the issue weeks ago. Again, is omission lying? I was convinced that him not saying anything aloud meant he was struggling and couldn't bear to tell me the truth. This enabled me to make every excuse available for his unruly behavior. I take full responsibility for that.

Finally, I got an answer. Luke was separated from his wife of many years. They were married young, and for the kids' sake, they slept in different rooms and went their separate ways. It was all new, so he didn't want to discuss it but assured me we were in the clear to continue this relationship. There were so many boundaries around what he could and couldn't do. I also had a list of growing things by the day of what I could not do anymore, being that sassy single that I once was.

Did I accept what he said as gospel? Did I want to believe this to be true? Completely!

Red flags were all around me, but I was so hooked on this man that I didn't see them or want to believe they were true. What we had was special. We met and had to be together—a love story of a lifetime. The timing sucked, but we were in it! Our situation would trump any marital rules, morals, and what was right and wrong. I was convinced of it.

And so, we continue. Mr. Who Never Told the Truth had boundaries, and I seemed to get more by the day. Just the way Luke wanted it and liked it.

Ask Yourself and Meaningful Journaling

This section is meant to reflect on your own story and thoughtfully reflect on your relationships.

___

___

___

Are you afraid to know the truth at times?

___

___

___

We sometimes do not want to face the music. Is there anything in your life you are unwilling to admit or face?

___

___

___

Is there someone who makes all the rules for you and wants to control your life?

____

____

____

Do you see any red flags? What are they? Can you tell someone or journal for further clarity?

____

____

____

DEREK MY NEW FRIEND, WE JUST HIT AN ALL-TIME LOW

I had seen Derek on several occasions in the presence of Luke. Derek is Luke's best friend. Derek loves the ladies, so I invited him out to ladies' night. If I could not see Luke in the evenings, especially on the weekends, I could do the next best thing and include his friend.

I decided to come clean with my two best girlfriends, Gloria and Karen, and tell them all about Luke. I thought Luke would appreciate including his friend in my night out so that he knew what I was up to. Derek asked if he could pick up Sergeant, my dog, and me, and drive us to Gloria's house.

The night started off wonderfully! As my besties and I do when together, we try on each other's clothes and typically come out with something fabulous from Gloria's closet that we take as our own. Derek enjoyed the fashion show we put on for him and the copious amounts of wine we typically drank.

We had a fantastic night. We all got along harmoniously and decided to play charades. Derek and I were on one team, and Gloria and Karen on the other. We played and laughed straight from our bellies. With many bottles of wine consumed, Derek and I stayed the night and slept on the couch.

We got up around 7:00 a.m. and were summoned home by a furious Luke. He wanted to meet at my house on a Saturday morning which was out of his typical schedule. We loaded Sergeant (my dog) into Derek's truck and drove to my house, where a furious Luke waited for us. He was livid, and I could not understand why. He was jealous that Derek and I spent the night with my friends and could not believe that I was that insensitive to his needs (and ego).

In my opinion, what better place to be than in the trusting hands of Luke's best friend? Luke berated me for an hour on how utterly inappropriate it was that I played charades and drank wine with Derek while he was cooped up in his own marital house with his "ex" wife. I was blown away and entirely confused. I could have been doing anything I wanted and chose to be in

the care of Luke's trusted friend, yet somehow, I was in the wrong.
His berating was relentless and extremely harsh. The more I questioned how I could be in the wrong in this situation while Luke was home with his wife, the angrier Luke was with me. How could I not understand where he was coming from? I felt helpless and ashamed. It was such a bizarre situation, and I felt threatened by the fact that Luke would end our charade at this point by exposing some of his true colours. Frankly, I was scared and did not want to be. I felt willing to end things with him given the abuse I took to defend my so-called horrendous actions.

Mr. Confusing left my house in a rage and went to work for the day. I was shaking, confused, and hurt as he drove off. I had no idea where I stood. I promised myself I would not allow him to treat me this way again. I felt entirely done until Luke called later that afternoon to apologize. He wanted to see me, to come over and talk. I agreed to see him. While I waited for Luke to arrive, I called Derek to try and comprehend what had happened through Derek's eyes. Derek wanted to stay out of it and did not want to be involved, which confused me even more.

When Luke arrived, he walked into my house sheepishly and wanted to explain how jealous he felt about me spending time with his friend when he could not see me. Was that even logical? I reasoned to myself that he must love me so much to make this much of a stink out of the situation. He asked me to forgive him for his harsh behaviour and wanted to spend some time with me. One thing led to another, and we ended up making love, and all seemed OK. I chalked this up to being a new couple just getting to know one another.

I'm afraid I was wrong.

Ask Yourself and Meaningful Journaling

This section is meant to reflect on your own story and thoughtfully reflect on your relationships.

___

___

___

Have you dealt with someone that is completely illogical?

So illogical that you question your sanity?

___

___

___

Were shamed and confused to the point that you can't understand how someone even arrived at that level of craziness?

____

____

____

SAVE YOUR SCISSORS

And the dance begins—the push and pull. There is endless waiting for a text, a call, a visit. I believed Luke and was being patient because I thought this was the best for his kids. That's what he told me anyway. Like a fish taking the bait, you never know what is at the end of the line. When in his presence, I was everything, and I loved that feeling. But everything I did now had conditions around it. I socially smoked at the time, so that was wrong. I apparently spent too much time with my friends, although later, Mr. Tell Me What to Do became friends with their husbands. He had the same effect on their husbands too, but the wives saw right through it.

Further on in my life, my favourite saying became "I would rather be lonely alone than alone with someone". This statement, although a cliché, ended up the truth that I live by and will for years to come.

I felt like a prisoner in a jail that I craved, addicted to what I thought was love. I felt like I was in charge, but I was under a spell that could not be lifted. I only did things now that would please him.

But like any trapped animal, I tried to flee the cage. I wondered what I was doing with my youth. I was young enough to have a life in a relationship that could include my own children and a future with some normalcy.

I started planning nights out with friends and had a wait-and-see attitude while hoping secretly for My Luke to sort out his life. As my nights out became more frequent, I started to pull away, to make myself scarce and to prioritize my well-being. I could always find something to do; there were plenty more fish in the sea. I started loving my time again and didn't feel I needed to report to Mr. Sergeant Take All the Space Up in My Mind. I began ignoring his calls and texts.

One night at a local bar, I was having a few beers, enjoying my freedom, and feeling so in charge of my life. The calls and texts were frantic, wondering where I was, what I was doing, and who I was with. I secretly enjoyed the torture I was putting him through. I wanted him to feel the way I felt night after night, wondering what was going on and how I fit into his life.

The local bar was close enough for me to walk home. At the end of the night, my best buddy David and I said our goodbyes and were ready to retire for the night. I unlocked the door and found Mr. Relentless Texter sitting at my kitchen table. The window screen was pushed out, and I realized at that moment that he had let himself in. Mr. Break & Enter was so worried about where I was and whether I was okay that he needed to break into my place to ensure my safety. How sweet, I thought. How crazy, I should have thought.

For weeks before and after this incident, I listened to one of my favourite songs by Dallas Green, called “Save your Scissors”. The lyrics read: “just save your scissors for someone else's skin; my surface is so tough; I don't think the blade will dig in; save your strength”.

The blade did dig in, more profoundly and deeply than I could have ever imagined.

Songwriters: Green Dallas John
Save Your Scissors lyrics © Emi April Music Inc., Bald Headed Boys Inc.

Ask Yourself and Meaningful Journaling

This section is meant to reflect on your own story and thoughtfully reflect on your relationships.

____

____

____

Have you ever felt like you were under a spell and couldn't see the truth?

____

____

____

Has someone ever violated your personal space and not questioned doing so?

____

____

____

WITHOUT A TRACE

What to do when you are trapped? RUN!

For an independent woman to feel so trapped is an insane feeling. Why did I not break up with him and move on? It's been about six months since I met Luke and I felt conflicted about the relationship, mostly because I was so confused. When someone talks from both sides of their mouth, it is hard to decipher what is going on. What I did know was that I needed to breathe. I needed to escape. I decided to move and take a break. When someone is consistently sucking you back in with words of love and admiration, it is hard to believe they don't love you. Every part of your being tells you that this behaviour is toxic, but your heart wants to believe, wants that love, and you can't seem to live without it.

I was going crazy, and nothing seemed rational. I decided to give notice in the apartment I was renting and escape to a friend's house. I sold most of my furniture and just wanted to hide from the world as a part of me was embarrassed to be in this situation. I felt I did not have any options, so I forged ahead with my plan. All was set. I negotiated my last day, had a place to stay where I could take my dog, and I could be set free.

Upon the move-out inspection with my property owner, he identified the broken kitchen window screen, and I was charged for the item. Again, no matter how much I wanted to break free, there were always dirty little reminders of my secret continuous abuse and emotional blackmail. In my confused state of mind, I reached out again to Mr. Break and Enter and said that I needed him to shell out the cash to pay for the window screen. Instantly Mr. Money Bags transferred money to pay for the damage. Was this a sign that our relationship could be salvaged because he was taking ownership of his irrational behaviour?

Stop Myriah! Just stop! My constant anticipation of wanting a different outcome was only frustrating me. Just move out and carry on. And so, I did!

Ask Yourself and Meaningful Journaling

This section is meant to reflect on your own story and thoughtfully reflect on your relationships.

____

____

____

Have you ever been embarrassed about the life you are living?

____

____

____

Have you recognized toxic behaviour but somehow felt it did not pertain to you? If you saw your best friend in a similar situation, you would likely 'smack them silly' but somehow your situation is different, meaningful in some way?

____

____

____

MY TIME AWAY – GLORIA'S HOUSE

I did it! I was all moved in snug as a bug under the roof of someone that wanted to protect me. I had my own room and washroom in a lovely house with a great friend that wanted nothing more than for me to be away from Mr. Controlling. We lived in a beautiful neighbourhood, and it was a serene place to reflect, walk my dog, and live peacefully while working on my career.

I had old friends visit that I was not allowed to have over in the past because Mr. Jealous didn't allow it. We partied and had a girl's night, then travelled to Phoenix, where my new roommate had a lovely place for us to stay.

My best friend from New York was able to visit, and we all hung out as carefree young women should.

I felt free, although my heart was missing HIM. I felt angry about how stupid I felt I had been to allow my life to get to this place. I felt lonely and drank enough wine to lessen the pain in my heart. I was embarrassed about run-ins I had had with friends and colleagues that stunk of dysfunction and vulgarity because of his presence.

I often asked how I got here. How does a nice girl get caught up in something that is so tumultuous?

For a few weeks, I was free. Free from feeling that I was the problem. Free from the feeling that I was always waiting for something to happen. Free from walking on eggshells. Free from being judged. Free from anxiety. Free from the tight grip of his control. Free to have a future that I wanted to lead and build for myself.

Ask Yourself and Meaningful Journaling

This section is meant to reflect on your own story and thoughtfully reflect on your relationships.

____

____

____

Why does a person long to be back with an individual that is so controlling?

____

____

____

You take a few steps forward and know it's the right thing but desperately want to fall back into old patterns? Why do you think this happens?

___

___

___

FOUND

Thankfully, I travelled a lot for business by air. I enjoyed flying for a few hours where nothing could touch you. There was no Wi-Fi on the plane, and I didn't need a reason not to be available. I could not be available. I still enjoy every second on a plane for that exact reason.

It had been about two months living with Gloria and I seemed to be moving on with my life. My job was good and I was travelling for work again. I was in Seattle, and my phone rang just before I was going to meet colleagues for dinner. It came from an unknown number and, much to my surprise, it was from Mr. From Whom I'm Hiding.

"Hello?", I answered.
"Oh hey, there you are," he says. It's Mr. Jekyll! Ack! What the heck am I thinking. "So how can I help you, Luke?".
"So, I just wanted to let you know that I bought a house," Luke reveals.

"Great," I say, "Good for you!"
Luke adds, "Um yeah, just wanted your input on the area I chose and type of place."
"Oh, so you already bought it?" I asked.
Luke says, "Yes!"
"Then why do you need my input?" I almost wanted to scream.
"Well, I just wanted to let you know." Luke explained.
"OK! Great, well, enjoy. I'm sure your kids will enjoy having a place of your own. OK. Bye!" I said feeling super empowered.

I got off the phone wondering why this guy is calling me for my input when the deal is done but yet wanting my insight on this done deal. Ha ha! But his plan worked. Now I am quasi excited that he has moved on, that he is moving out of his family home.

Does that mean that we will be moving forward too? That we can be together? Was me moving on and hiding from him the catalyst for him not wanting to lose me?

Oh, the cycle starts again. The false hope, the thoughts of the future, the getting rustled right in—such a vicious cycle. Stay strong, Myriah! You are out!

Stay out! You have set your boundary. Now stick to it! Do not fall back into his power and control. But he loves me. He has made some progress. Why would he find it so important to call me from another number to tell me he bought a house? A home for us? A home so that we can have a life together.

His last word from that call is that we should talk.

Ask Yourself and Meaningful Journaling

This section is meant to reflect on your own story and thoughtfully reflect on your relationships.

____

____

____

We all know better, but the heart wants what the heart wants. Why do we always feel like giving someone the benefit of the doubt when the situation doesn't lend itself to it?

____

____

____

We feel that the slightest reach out means that someone has seen the light and we feel like we were the catalyst for this change. Why?

____

____

____

LET'S BUY FURNITURE

Within two weeks of receiving that call in Seattle, I am now taking calls from Mr. I'm Moving Forward. I feel like I am sneaking around Gloria, my lovely friend who allowed me to escape Luke to live with her. Luke thought it best that I didn't mention that we were seeing each other again, and I complied.

Luke is excited about moving into the new house. There are lovely rooms for his sons in a three-level townhouse with a nice deck in the yard surrounded by mature trees. Oh, the fun we could have at this house!

Luke started asking me to come furniture shopping with him so I could have some input on the décor. To be honest, I was there to be there. Luke made all the significant decisions, and, although he was paying for all his furniture, it was so important that I had a "say." It's funny reflecting on this time and knowing that I am an intelligent person and not seeing right through this type of behaviour. Again, I felt like I was under a spell and had no control over my brain's left or right side.

As you can guess, as Mr. I Make All the Decisions moved in, the stay-over parties started slowly but consistently. Again, I was lying to myself and now to Gloria about my whereabouts and how I was spending my time. My friends would not have been impressed that I made all this effort to "hide," and now how easily I am found and right back in Luke's clutches.

Ultimately, my friends were not stupid and knew exactly what was happening. Since I sold most of my furniture and belongings when I decided to go into hiding, I didn't have much to lose. It seemed like a perfect option for me to reestablish myself in his new home. I filled his bed every night but stayed at Gloria's on the weekends and the weeknights his sons were there.

We spent our free nights going for fun dinners, enjoying drinks, and talking endlessly about Luke's business and his desires. My career and aspirations were not as important in the grand scheme as Mr. I Rule Everything. At the time, I still believed there were traditionally male and female roles, and I sat perfectly happy in the backseat, letting Luke steer us on whatever journey he was on.

Ask Yourself and Meaningful Journaling

This section is meant to reflect on your own story and thoughtfully reflect on your relationships.

___

___

___

Hiding information from your friends and loved ones typically means or feels that something is wrong. Are you currently hiding anything from loved ones?

___

___

___

Why do you think that we often surrender our power, hopes and dreams to please our partner?

____

____

____

MEET THE KIDS

While I was still at Gloria's, I took a part-time job marketing and selling cosmetics for a marketing company. I thought taking extra work would keep me occupied and perhaps give me more purpose so that I could have the strength to stay away from Mr. I Plan on Ruining Your Life. Because we were in contact, I let Luke know I had a shift at a local cosmetic store demonstrating colour matching foundation. This is funny because I never wore foundation and did not know much about it, but this part-time gig served its purpose and kept me busy and away from totally letting Luke consume my life.

Low and behold, one day I am doing my thing and in walks Luke in tow with his very adorable little boys. Mr. I Could Win an Oscar for the amount of acting he did is VERY surprised to run into a friend at a cosmetic store of all places! Me!

Look, boys, this is daddy's "friend" Myriah. "I didn't know you worked here?" Like fuck you didn't know that I was there. I couldn't catch my breath, though. These lovely, sweet boys stood in front of me, and I asked their names and how they were doing. I showed them how this magical foundation starts off white and when I rubbed it into their hands, its colour shifted to match their skin tone. Magic, just like their dad running into a friend haphazardly at the store. Bravo, everyone! Bravo!

However, I was reminded in a text after they left how important it was to him that I meet his sons. They were his pride and joy and since I was so important to him, I guess it made sense that I was privileged to be on the other side of this introduction.

We were making progress, I guess. I stayed with Luke most of the evenings in his bed and new home, and now I was casually introduced to the loves of his life. I was convinced again we were meant to be and that he was taking every step possible to forge a future with me. He reminded me many times how he was taking all these risks to make me feel that we had a solid relationship. He was the hero always!

It took a few weeks, but the subsequent encounter occurred when we decided to meet again with the kids and walk our dogs. This innocent dog walk allowed him to coincidentally run into his friend Myriah, therefore providing another "chance" encounter with the kids.

In their childlike ways, the boys greeted me with kindness and innocence. I introduced them to Sergeant, my 100 lb. dog, large in size and giant in heart. He was a gentle soul and wonderful to everyone he met. However, the oldest of the kids was terrified of Sergeant and started crying. I knew in my heart of hearts that he was not only afraid of Sergeant. I think he intuitively knew this was the end of his mom and dad's relationship, and that I was the conflict in that relationship. We cut the visit short as I wanted this little boy to feel better, so we all went on our merry way until the next time.

As it turned out, I finally ended up "living" in the basement and became a fixture in Luke's house. This was easy to explain to the kids as to why I was there when they came for their weekly visits. At bedtime, when the boys stayed over, everyone went to their rooms (me to my room in the basement), and these young kids had dad time.

Eventually, I was the last person they saw at night and the first person they saw in the morning when I moved upstairs and into daddy's bed. This was by design (mine, of course). I wanted them to trust that I would never interfere in their relationship with their father.

I loved seeing the boys on a regular basis. They were lovely in so many ways. We bonded and became a family. While we were together, there were no issues, no relationship dysfunction, and we were on our way to moving on with our lives.

But were we?

Ask Yourself and Meaningful Journaling

This section is meant to reflect on your own story and thoughtfully reflect on your relationships.

____

____

____

Have you ever been made to feel that someone is making every effort to please you and that you should feel so much gratitude, but that person is just doing the basics of what should be done in a relationship?

____

____

____

Why in some situations do we not expect more from ourselves and let our partner rule the relationship?

____

____

____

FAMILY VACATION

This was one incident that really struck my therapist, years later. We joked on how she should pay me to come for continuous visits as she never knew what would come out of my mouth next.

Mr. Entrepreneur was making a name for himself. His business grew swiftly and exponentially. Orders were coming in; he hired the industry's best and had damn good instincts in growing the business. Luke expanded quickly as there was a need for his equipment in Mexico, so travel became frequent in his life. As previously mentioned, I too travelled for work. Luke and I had so many fights about this. Apparently, I wasn't there enough for him, and things didn't get done around the house because of my absence. He could not understand the appeal of work travel, until HE THE LORD and SAVIOUR started travelling. Once he did, he could not get enough of it. I thought at the time it was because he was just a hypocrite, but it went way further than that.

When Mr. I Hated Myriah Travelling started travelling himself, I was okay with it. I lived full time in our house and took the kids when Luke couldn't. I was happy being a stepmom. Luke told me he had to go to Florida for a week for business, and I was all good with that. He left under the guise that he had some serious business to look after. Luke called me every day around dinner time, just after he called his kids as he would every day. I will say that Luke was, and I'm sure still is, a good dad. I was just added to the roster after saying goodnight to his boys, and the week went on (or so I thought).

Luke returned home, and we had the boys for dinner the following week. I'm sure he missed them dearly as I missed him. I made dinner while Luke picked up the boys from their mom's house, and I set the table and looked forward to us all being together again.

When they arrived, we sat down to chat about school and our week, and then detailed stories started pouring out of the kids' mouths about their family time in Florida last week. I was confused because I didn't know they went with their mom to Florida. Wait for it - they not only went to Florida with their mom, but they also went as a family and with their neighbourhood friends and kids too! What the actual FUCK? I could have screamed. I heard delightful stories about dad's fun in the pool with them. How he won a beer-drinking contest and how wonderful it was to be around their friends for a week. I honestly could not believe what I was hearing. In my personal childhood household, a united front in front of us kids was the foundation of my parent's relationship. So, I smiled, and the boys continued to discuss their extraordinary adventures while I almost choked on a piece of tortellini with cream sauce. I told them how wonderful this all seemed and smiled pleasantly at their father. I always enjoyed having these beautiful boys around, but tonight I could not WAIT for them to have a bath and go to bed.

Bath time this night and prep for bed seemed like an eternity. I am sure Luke was happy that these next two hours seemed like a week in burning hell for me.

Luke volunteered to handle bedtime duties on his own while I cleaned up. I was so confused. Again, I thought, did I miss something? Did I hear his plans wrong? Was

I not paying attention to what he was planning? Because how could all this have unfolded without me knowing, and how could Mr. Liar Liar Pants on Fire lie to my face so easily and beautifully?

I can still remember it like it was yesterday. I sat on the floor in the living room patiently waiting for Luke to come down to face his deceit and lies. He casually walked in as if nothing had happened and did not even offer to explain. He went to the kitchen, got a drink, and then decided to join me. How calm could this motherfucker be, I thought?

I said to him, did you want to explain what happened at dinner time and how you could lie to me so blatantly about something like this? With the calmest voice, he said that I would not have understood the need for this vacation and that he was protecting ME by not telling me in advance. This was the best for everyone, and I was not in a position to deny his boys this experience with their mom and dad. So back on me. My fault. My lack of understanding and attitude made him need to concoct this story so that he could protect me and my feelings. WOW! Just WOW!

Here we were again, with me as the terrible person who made him do all these things so that he could protect me and win father of the year at the same time.

I should have slapped his lying mother fucking face and walked straight out of there. I knew I wasn't the type of person he seemed to think I was. If Luke told me he wanted this for his boys, I would have accepted this and would not have put up too much of a roadblock. But I was left feeling inadequate because somehow it was my fault that I could not handle the truth, and his only sin was protecting my heart.

I stayed.

Ask Yourself and Meaningful Journaling

This section is meant to reflect on your own story and thoughtfully reflect on your relationships.

____

____

____

When you are lied to so obviously, how can you not see the real issue? How is it that this became a 'me' problem and twisted back on me so easily?

____

____

____

Why do we stay in these situations?

____

____

____

MY MOTHER LOVES HIM

At this point in my life, I had been away from my hometown of Chicago for ten years. My parents had never been to visit me. My father had been diagnosed with a terminal illness and lived only a few months after being diagnosed. My Mom was on her own. Around this time, I oversaw planning Luke's grand opening party for a building he bought to continue his company's growth. Things were humming along. Sales were good, money seemed to be rolling in, and more change was inevitable.

Luke wanted a big grand opening party where no expense was spared. The budget was $200K, and he wanted a big-ticket band to play. They were a popular country band and most of the Denver old town cowboys loved that genre of music. A $60K price tag, but this was suitable for the type of party this was. I recently completed my Event Management Certificate from the local college and planning for this type of event was big for me. So big, that when I think back to it now, it is insane that I did this almost single-handedly and created such an experience that some people in the city will never forget it. Valet parking, red carpet, a step and repeat with champagne, Marche style food and a host bar. Luke invited my mother to attend, which, of all things, could not have warmed my heart more. He offered to pay for her ticket, had a driver pick her up, and she stayed with us at our house. The night of the event, he paid for her hotel room. My mother had no idea that a party like this could ever exist. She was in the wild west now, and there is nothing like a megalomaniac manufacturing clientele shit-kicking party.

As we were getting ready that afternoon, Luke had gone shopping with his father to get a few last-minute items. I loved it when he spent time with his father. When they returned to our house, I was presented with a beautiful necklace from Nordstrom. A silver spiral egg-shaped pendant with a chain. It was gorgeous. This was a gift for all the arduous work I put into this night and a token of his appreciation. I can say that Luke always surprised me with extraordinary gifts and had immaculate taste. Years later, I wonder if all these gifts were guilt presents to ease his conscience. He always loved the way I received gifts. Whether it was a chocolate bar or a Dolce and Gabbana watch, I accepted any with a world of gratitude. So many things would have been easier if I understood the complicated nuances of narcissism at the time.

When my mother witnessed such thoughtful, beautiful acts of kindness, and generosity, she could not help but love Luke. Luke made so many lovely gestures toward my mother. He would make a memorable trip upstairs at bedtime to ensure she was comfortable and happy. My mother was over the moon with Luke and loved that I had this man by my side.

Back at the party, things were in full swing when we arrived. Guests were arriving, and the buzz in the building was palpable. People were excited to see this appliance manufacturing sweetheart succeed and grow his business so rapidly. The manufacturing facility was transformed into the vibe of a cool nightclub. Prosecco and appetizers served, pictures being flashed all over the place, and an entire stage in the main section with back line promised a night of fabulous music and dancing.

I hired a coordinator to look after the specifics of the evening so that I could enjoy the night and feel free to celebrate with Luke. But the absence of Luke for extended periods left me with a nagging feeling that not everything was on the up and up. When I finally spotted Luke across the room, he was with his Customer Service team, mostly one employee specifically. I had a nagging feeling that made me want to shout. Even though I could not explain my gut instinct, I wasn't going to let anything ruin my night, this glorious party, having my mom with me and basking in an event planned and executed so well.

I confronted Luke when we got back to the hotel room about his mysterious absences from the party and with whom he had been. Like countless other times, I was going crazy and not seeing things as they were. He was gone for hours on end, and I couldn't understand the need to spend an inordinate amount of time with his employees. Was I going mad? Am I crazy? If this perfect man is telling me that I'm seeing things that are not there and annoyed that I would mutter such nonsense, then I guess I am either insecure or a touch on the crazy side. I must work harder on being a better person for Mr. Perfect.

Ask Yourself and Meaningful Journaling

This section is meant to reflect on your own story and thoughtfully reflect on your relationships.

____

____

____

Have you been in a situation where everything landed on your lap? Where someone made you feel that every situation or question was only because you were insecure and seeing things that were not there?

____

____

____

MOMMY DEAREST

Mr. Perfect does not have the perfect role model. Mom abandoned her very young kids to marry an accountant from her work. She left her husband to fend for himself as a single father of three small kids. Knowing this story always made me think I should be more sensitive to Luke and his needs, because abandonment can cause many traumatic life issues if not dealt with at some point. Sometimes when Luke acted like a jerk or was plain mean, I made excuses for him because of the way his mom left with no regard for him or his siblings. The other two kids struggled at some point with addiction. Luke stayed out of this arena. In fact, he always looked after his siblings when push came to shove and when their lifestyle issues reared their ugly heads. Luke and his dad went to the rescue most times to see how they could help; they often ended up enabling them as that was the only way they knew how to deal with these problems and show love and support.

Like that cat who came back, Mommy Dearest showed up in these kids' lives with a new stepsister and her new husband in tow. The expectation was that she and her entourage would be welcomed back with open arms. A mother's emotional blackmail can take hold of even the strongest people.

It surprised me to find out that mommy lived within walking distance of the house that Luke bought. And on that glorious day when I had the opportunity to be introduced to this person, they walked into our backyard as if mommy was the pillar of motherhood. She was a harsh-looking woman. She looked like she lived a life of trying to defend her horrendous actions, while deep down trying to live with the guilt and regret of ruining her small children's lives. How does one do that?

I was brought up to respect your parents, and I will extend the same to Mommy Dearest. We had superficial fun at times, enjoying BBQs, wine, and good banter. But all good things come to an end. Mommy Dearest, as it turns out, likes to indulge a little too much and becomes quite a mean person.

Mommy would come by often and seemed to want to claim her stake in her son's life, and, somehow, I believe she thought I was a threat. She blamed all her son's actions on me. Most of the time, I had no idea what I was being blamed for, but I was the target, nonetheless. I have zero tolerance for this type of behaviour (but I put up with her son's for so long which is still very curious to me). Although I desperately wanted to bond with this woman, it was a relationship in which I could not participate. I put up with her bullying and tantrums because she was Mr. Abandoned at Childhood's Mother, and hoped that one day Luke would come to his own conclusion about her. But this toxic behaviour is so unhealthy that it could kill an army of saints.

Luke's father was one of the best humans I had ever met, and his second wife was an angel. She took on an entire family at an early age and mothered them like they were her own. They were a hardy couple that enjoyed each other's company, tried to tuck Mommy Dearest's unforgivable decisions behind them, and did their best to function like a family full of love and kindness. That was evident to me from the moment I met them—a home where there were open arms and hearts. I am sure that Mommy Dearest despised this, and it showed.

On the day of the big launch party, Mommy Dearest was one of the first guests to show up. In their beautiful ways, Dad and stepmom were always such a part of Luke's and now my life. They supported Luke in his entrepreneurial journey, encouraged him every step of the way, and were well-liked and welcomed in his workplace. No one knew Mommy Dearest, so I'm not surprised she was the first to arrive and stake her claim. Funnily enough, she wrote, "Mommy Dearest" on her name tag!

First in, first out is a thing, and that is exactly what happened at that party. Mommy Dearest got shitfaced before all the guests even arrived and became super belligerent. It was my distinct pleasure to ensure security escorted her off the premises and home. So sad.

From that evening on, I was doomed; Mommy Dearest blamed all Luke's lousy decisions on me. However, I was not a materialistic person, and when Luke purchased his mini-mansion and started collecting expensive cars, it was my doing, of course. It was my fault when Mr. Liar Liar Pants on Fire didn't call his mommy, my fault when invites were not extended, or when future parties were held at our house without an invite. I'm sure I was blamed for all the ladies Luke fucked too. My fault!

Ask Yourself and Meaningful Journaling

This section is meant to reflect on your own story and thoughtfully reflect on your relationships.

____

____

____

How do you handle family dynamics when a loved one tries to sabotage your relationship?

____

____

____

What do you do when a parent, guardian or family member has not dealt with their own past issues, and it affects the entire family dynamic?

____

____

____

LOST IN LAS VEGAS

Vegas is a fun place! And I got to do some fun travel for work – an infomercial conference is a good time. I decided to invite Mr. I Love Gambling on my Vegas trip. I had the hotel room, and all Luke needed to do was fly down and enjoy the festivities. I now worked for a media company that sold advertising, and we rolled with some great people. This trip would give Luke time to get to know my GM and leadership group, and we could do some fun things on my turf for a change since everything was always around Mr. I Need to be the Centre of the Universe.

There was never a dull moment at these conferences. We were invited to some of the best parties, ate at some of the best restaurants, and enjoyed Viva Lost Wages! I honestly was excited to enjoy time with Luke away from the daily hustle and wanted him to respect what I do for a living. I worked on the conference floor for two days. Luke was coming down for the parties and group dinners, and then we planned on renting a car and driving to the Hoover Dam.

A plan is only a plan, though, until it is realized. I hoped it would be, but, again, it was not. Thinking back on how mortified I was about his behaviour and lack of respect for me, my life was laughable and devastating at the same time.

Imagine your boss, colleagues, and peers at a planned dinner, and your partner does not show up as expected. Imagine your partner making excuses about where he was and why he wasn't sitting at the seat beside me in the spot with his name on a place card. Imagine sitting there humiliated because everyone else's partners were there, and you cannot fathom why yours was absent. It was a mixed bag of 'is he safe or is he the world's biggest jerk'? I hated this jackass right then, I could not connect with him via his cell phone, text, or pigeon carrier, just missing in action and nowhere to be found. But, as you see the pattern here, there was no need for any explanation, an excuse was made for everything, and the kicker of it all is somehow it was me not being clear on what the plan was and what it meant to me. I should have told him this was our plan, that everyone would be there. How could he know, Mr. Ignorant and

Innocent? I was not communicative enough to parlay a simple dinner invite to ensure that his attendance is required. FUCK! I was humiliated and disgusted by him at that moment.

I'm not done with this night yet! So, I decided to carry on my merry way with a smile on my face like nothing was wrong. My colleagues and I visited a few piano bars, went on a roller coaster in New York, New York, and did some shopping at the Harley Davidson shop. It was time to go home as I still had work to do at the conference the following day—still no word from Mr. Missing in Action. I went to the hotel room and am now worried sick. Where could he be? What could he be doing? Was he safe? It was his first time in Las Vegas; what was I supposed to think? I decided to go to bed, but sleep was nowhere in my future because I was just fueled by angst and anger. Bing! My text message alert goes off. It was from Mr. I Don't Give a Fuck About Your Feelings. Wait for it! It was a picture of a 1,000-dollar chip that I'm guessing he won. I couldn't even fathom what was going through that brain of his. Was this $1000 chip to make up for my humiliation and utter disappointment from this evening? I did not respond. Bing!

Another notification, again from Luke.

Another picture of the chip! I could not give a damn. Bing! Bing! Bing! Notification after notification. Where am I, why aren't I answering him, where am I?

Fuck him! Now the desperate help call comes in. He's lost and doesn't know where he is. He needs my help, he's helpless. Oh, this makes sense now; you were temporarily delusional and lost your memory and any motor skills you had. We were staying at the Paris hotel, right across the street from the Bellagio where he was. Granted, regular blocks and Las Vegas blocks are not measured equally. He was just across the street but couldn't find his way. I had to get dressed and now go on a mission to find Mr. Lost in Las Vegas. I booked it across the street and found him drunk and walking toward the Paris hotel. I had to escort his lying and drunk ass to the room so he could rest and savour in the fruits of his gambling and intoxication. I could not make this up! Nothing more could be said about him standing me up because he was drunk and lost, and because he was the one that was compromised somehow. And by the way, he still had the $1000 winnings. Good for you, Mr. I'm Starting to Hate You!

Ask Yourself and Meaningful Journaling

This section is meant to reflect on your own story and thoughtfully reflect on your relationships.

____

____

____

Why do we feel we have to make excuses for our partners' bad behaviour? Is this something you've done or are currently doing? Why do you feel you have to do this?

____

____

____

We often feel that we have to fix someone or take on a 'project' when selecting our partners. Have you done this? If so, why did you feel you needed to?

____

____

____

WORKING WITH THE MISTRESS

Do you ever feel so blind that you wonder what planet you live on? It's a strange existence living and loving a person with so many issues. You believe them wholeheartedly. I am unsure if I did not want to see the signs and red flags or just chose not to. I seemed to be living in a dreamland and not seeing all the things happening around me: case in point.

There was a Customer Service Manager that worked with Luke. Cute as a button, but I never for a moment was worried about this new hire. Luke made me feel like the centre of his universe as he talked out of both sides of his mouth. I was confident in our life and situation. I always said to Luke that if for whatever reason he found someone else that he wanted to be with that, you clean your "house" first and then pursue something else. I think that is respectful and fair. He never expressed any want or need to do so, and often reminded me how well he treated me, so in my mind I never had any reason to worry. I never felt I needed to snoop on my man's phone or otherwise because I expected mutual respect. Mistake!

I worked with Luke from the beginning of his entrepreneurial journey to helping with the event, with branded promotional items, and with miscellaneous projects. Although Luke presented this like he was helping me, it was another way to control the situation if I were to look back and be honest about it. As you recall from a previous chapter, at the grand opening party, Luke was spending a ridiculous amount of time with one of his employees.

There was a job fair where the local trade college was looking for companies to participate in the potential hiring of students in future roles. Luke asked me to work with the Customer Service Manager to help set up the booth and participate in the event. This was with Ms. I'm Not Having an Affair with Your Man. We worked together on this project to fruition, and perhaps in my very naïve ways, I still didn't think anything was happening between them. To be honest, maybe I did not want to see what was happening to my world, but I didn't think it would be that blatant. After the trade show, I delivered some of the items left over from the booth and returned them to Ms. Customer Service Bitch All Over My Boyfriend's Ass's office. I noticed that her office was rearranged and efficiently organized. She quickly told me that Luke suggested these great ideas, and that he was instrumental in making these significant changes to the functionality of the space. I'd be lying if, for a moment, I didn't feel a tiny twinge of "that's curious". However, I had so much faith in our journey and life together that I didn't give too much light to my intuition.

In hindsight, a huge mistake.

I will revisit this situation in a future chapter.

Ask Yourself and Meaningful Journaling

This section is meant to reflect on your own story and thoughtfully reflect on your relationships.

___

___

___

We sometimes turn a blind eye to the obvious tell-tale signs that something is not on the up and up. Should we explore all of our instincts, no matter how uncomfortable?

Are there things right now that you should question or explore further in your relationship?

Should we blindly trust our partners? Do you blindly trust?

HANGING WITH HIS MANAGER'S WIFE, MISTRESS NUMBER TWO

When I look back now, I wonder if I was blind! Mr. Innocent that Never Did Anything Wrong was always full of stories and excuses.

We were a social couple, and we would also plan quiet dinners for the two of us. At some point, we would have the entire restaurant sucked into our tomfoolery; we could entertain a group full of people and start a party faster than you could light a match. I did love this part of us, however, at some point I felt that Luke was always trying to compete for the spotlight. I would back off because I thought he needed it more than I did. Perhaps I was enabling this behaviour, but I told myself I didn't need the attention as much as I thought he might.

Don't get me wrong, I love the spotlight and am a natural extrovert with, some would say, a good sense of humour mixed with a massive dose of innuendo. Luke was rich with it also and would sometimes 'reach the limit' and go overboard. Often, because he was paying the bill, people just put up with his behaviour. However, he was the most hilarious person to be around. He had a light-hearted boyish charm about him that was super infectious. I love a gregarious, outgoing human being, particularly of the male persuasion.

I can see why women were attracted to him. He would make you feel like a million dollars and an essential part of his surroundings. We had one woman that was always in our orbit. It happened to be the wife of one of Luke's managers, an attractive girl that always seemed to be on our fringe. Never directly invited but always there. Luke would explain that, because she was one of the manager's wives, she was always present. He would describe her as a nuisance but somehow always put up with her. I particularly could not tolerate her, and she was always close, not up close and personal, but always nearby. We often could not shake her, and she was always lurking around. Quite hilarious, but again I never felt fully threatened by her presence. That was likely because Luke always had great reasons and explanations, but also kept me in the "queen" zone, so I felt he would never betray me. I am sure women and men in this position have felt the same way. I would have bet a million dollars that Luke and I were solid, and there was no mischievous behaviour held in his court.

I always wondered why this leech's husband never minded his wife hanging around his boss. Often, we would see curious behaviour with this woman flirting openly with Luke's customers. I mean to each their own, but I silently judged how they lived their married life and glad my partner was not like that (Ha!) But the consistent existence of this person in our social life was sometimes unbearable. I didn't like her as a person, and I would never choose this person as a friend of mine. However, looking back at it now it all tracks. I will end this chapter the same way as I did the previous one. I will revisit this situation in a future chapter. It will all make sense.

Ask Yourself and Meaningful Journaling

This section is meant to reflect on your own story and thoughtfully reflect on your relationships.

____

____

____

Are you setting boundaries for yourself in your relationship? If so, what are they?

____

____

____

Should we set boundaries for others? If so, what does that look like?

____

____

____

THE FLIGHT

So many nights, Luke's cell phone died, or he lost it or lost track of time.

I remember coming home from a business trip, and I was so sick. Luke did show up to pick me up from the airport; he had a few drinks, may I add. However, he showed up and drove me home, only to leave as soon as he dropped me off. I was so mad. I felt it would have been nice for him to stay with me, but he convinced me that this was important business and he had to leave and continue with his meeting at 10:00 pm. I did express my disappointment; however, it fell on deaf ears. I decided to take a bath and go to bed as I hadn't felt that bad in so long. I was woken up to my cell phone ringing, likely at 1:00 am. It was Luke, he ran out of gas and was stuck somewhere in the middle of bum fuck nowhere and needed my help.

I was sick, and although he dumped my ass off earlier, now he wanted me to bail him out. I was beside myself, but as you might have guessed, I got dressed and went off to save my Mr. Not So Knight in Shining Armour. I was so mad and felt so used. I felt like I was in a trance and always needing to please this person although his actions were not always reciprocated.

I was a free woman, and I was not held hostage, but still I went. And of course, when he did pick me up from the airport and leave me when I was sick, he was actually doing me the ultimate favour by taking time out of his "business" meeting to make time for me. It was such emotional blackmail. I was attracted to him sexually, and he just knew how to control me enough to allow every manipulation. I was always made to feel he was superior to me, but I now realize I was special, and he was the inferior one. Many people I have talked to since my escape from this situation have had the same experience. It's so fascinating how the strongest of the strong can be manipulated into submission by these people. You want to be loved and accepted by them, but you can't seem to do enough for them.

One night, Luke was travelling somewhere on a plane. Again, I am of the mindset that if you do something nefarious, you make your bed and deal with the consequences. However, in our relationship, I felt that I had to accommodate all the bad behaviour because everything somehow was my fault.

At that time, Wi-Fi was only just made available on some airlines. Luke often would pay for this service to get some work done and bid his sons goodnight when he was travelling. On this particular day, my understanding was that Luke was in the air, and my phone rang sometime around 1:00 am. It was Luke. He said something was wrong with the flight and that he thought they might be in jeopardy. He told me he loved the boys and me, and that he wanted me to know this, should anything happen, and then hung up the phone. What does one do when you think your loved one is going down in a horrific plane disaster and you have no control? I was never in control of anything from the moment I met this man. How does one go to sleep with this knowledge? I started googling flight paths and looking for any emergency issues reported. I thought the worst but was also relieved that I was the one Luke contacted for his farewell call. I was weirdly flattered but devastated at the same time. Was this how I was going to lose the love of my life? I didn't know what to do. The rest of the morning was me pondering, wondering, scared out of my mind, devastated in thinking the worst, and curious about what was happening. I can't tell you how often I worried in the middle of the night because so many things happened to this person when he was expected home.

Was I the most gullible person to keep believing all these trash excuses? When I got off the call from the plane with the near-death possible outcome, I wondered at one point, "Was this call meant for me"? Was he actually on a plane?" The next day, I still could not find any record of any travel emergency where a plane or equipment was compromised. I would research this for hours trying to find evidence that his claims were valid, but how do you question the veracity of someone's near-death experience? It seems unreasonable that I would even ask for confirmation of some sort. Right?

False! Luke was fine the morning after, no tragic accident happened and when asked later that day, it wasn't a big deal. End of conversation. I was just going crazy as usual!

Ask Yourself and Meaningful Journaling

This section is meant to reflect on your own story and thoughtfully reflect on your relationships.

____

____

____

Can things ever get so ridiculous in your relationship that you can't figure out what is real or imagined? Does your partner help you clarify through effective communication what the actual issues are?

____

____

____

ALONE IN A BIG HOUSE

In a house more gorgeous than most can imagine, three hundred- and sixty-degree views of the mountains perched high on a hill in a gated community. "In love" with the man of my "dreams" and acting stepmom, which I loved more than anything in my life. What more could a girl want? Having 'everything' though, doesn't eliminate loneliness. On the outside, the house, cars, expensive handbags, and being in a "successful" relationship. On the inside, vulnerable, lonely, second-guessing, loss of oneself, and devastated, this is the reality.

I remember thinking I would rather be lonely alone than lonely in a relationship. It hurts less. At this point in my life, I spent most of my time alone, running a large household, always trying to prove myself to someone I should never have bowed down to. I lost myself and wasn't sure who I was. I was a solid up-and-comer working on her career who had a lot of friends and acquaintances. Yet, I felt like a slave to my lifestyle and my relationship. I worked constantly and spent so much time in solitude in that big house. I daydreamed about Luke proposing to me and tried to visualize what that might look like. I loved being a stepmom and the "life" I became accustomed to.

I remember begging in my heart that Luke would just come home, spend time with me and be a family. It's hilarious that I didn't think he would be spending time sneaking around with others the way we started in our relationship. There is a saying, "once a cheater, always a cheater," and those of us who were the mistress think that would never happen to us. Earlier I used the term sneaking around. For the record, I don't think there was any sneaking around. Luke's arrogance would not allow that. I believe he felt that he didn't need to sneak around. He was above that. Luke did what he wanted with whom he wanted and just left those he discarded in the dust.

No one feels sorry for a person that cries alone in her massive living quarters, taking baths in huge tubs overlooking the mountains with the ability to have a steam shower and to prepare meals on the best appliances with a kitchen grander than some people's apartments. Poor me, I had everything. Who do you talk to about this type of thing? Why would one complain? And perhaps because I didn't want to see what was happening in my own life and around me, I didn't seek out any answers or support.

I feel that we get trapped in the perception of oneself. We get tied into what society thinks success looks like. We lose sight of our 'why' and intention for our own life and tend to get lost in other people's (husbands, partners, family) wants and dreams. Can two people live harmoniously together and keep their identity and sense of self? All rhetorical, of course.

It is tough to climb out of this space when you are at a loss and in the clouds where you have no sense of reality.

I was swimming in a 6-year pool of narcissism that left me powerless, questioning what and where I was at this time in my life.

And every step of the way, when I questioned my lifeline and partner, I was made to feel that I was wrong, crazy, unstable, and insecure.

Ask Yourself and Meaningful Journaling

This section is meant to reflect on your own story and thoughtfully reflect on your relationships.

____

____

____

At what point do we ask for help or seek therapy?

____

____

____

How do we keep our own identity in our relationship?

___

___

___

Is it time to regain one thing in your life that you feel you should revisit or regain?

___

___

___

THE CELL PHONE

Mr. I'm Never Home Anymore makes me feel like I'm crazy. Even though every bone in my body says something is so wrong with my relationship, my partner tells me everything is in my head. I would hear things like "we just live busy lives" or "things will settle down eventually". I was always looking sideways at him.

He would leave that house every day with the dry cleaning ready. I always had everything prepared for him, in a place that was always ready for guests and ready for action, but no one, including Luke, was ever there. The only time I could count on was when the boys were with us on the weekend, unless there was an emergency at work, which happened often.

I just had enough of it. I knew I wasn't crazy or blind at this point anymore, but where could I get conclusive answers? There was a magical box called his smartphone that Luke never lost sight of. It never rested anywhere but, in his pocket, hand, or under his pillow.

There must be a plethora of information and evidence on that phone. Since he was never without it, how could I get it? I started plotting ways of getting my paws on it. I could not stop thinking about how I could find some information that would give me a clue that I wasn't one foot away from being admitted into a psych institute.

One night, as usual, Mr. Don't Look at my Phone came home after a few drinks and went to bed. It was late, and I could not sleep. I was so livid with him, and I finally had enough of his bullshit. I got out of the bed and walked around to his side. We had a massive California king bed, it seemed to take forever until I got around to his side. As always, the phone was charging and safely tucked under his pillow. I called his name, and he did not stir. I grabbed the cord, and I pulled it ever so gently. It slid easily out from under the pillow, over the mattress, and it into my hands. My heart was pounding so hard. I was scared this was a defying, and defining, moment.

I do not know what would have happened if he caught me looking at his phone. I can tell you that in ordinary circumstances, I would NEVER disrespect anyone by looking into their private messages and communications. But I felt that I did not have any options at this point. Either I was going crazy, or Mr. Liar Liar Pants on Fire would get busted. I snuck into our laundry room, which was adjacent to our walk-in closet but had a pocket door that slid shut. My excellent plan did not include prior knowledge of his password to get into the vault of lies, but I had a few options I could try. The first number combination I used was our house alarm security code. I could not believe my eyes! I was IN!

I thought I was going to throw up. I was never that scared in my life. I felt like a trembling child waiting for my father's wrath if we did something wrong as a kid. I needed to do this, but I didn't want to be wrong about my instinct and find out that I have been a terrible accusing person for so long. I wanted to feel I was the same person I was years ago before I met Mr. I Will Ruin Your Life.

The first place I was going to check was his text messages. Boom! There it was. I thought it might take more than a second to find the dirty truth. I was devastated, relieved, sad, broken, disgusted, scared, and vindicated at that moment. The first message I read was from Ms. Customer Service Manager, the one with whom I just finished a work project as per Luke's instruction. The statement said, "I feel like a teenager whenever we are together, and I look forward to us travelling together. I love you". Blood was rising to my head, and I thought my head was going to blow off. I could not breathe; I thought I was going to faint. How did I not see this coming?

The second message was from the wife of Luke's manager, with intimate words and expressing there was no doubt they had some kind of relationship far more significant than being the wife of an employee.

One of the messages read something to the effect of wondering when he was going to tell "Myriah" of all the things that were going on and that sooner than later would be ideal. ACK! How is this happening? I guess deep down, I knew, but did not want to see it. Mr. I Speak From Both Sides of My Mouth made me feel like

I was going mad but so many things were happening that suggested otherwise.

There was one more message with a name that I didn't recognize; it was from a girl in Florida. She was wondering when he would return to town and said that she couldn't wait to see him.

That was enough! I didn't need to see anymore! I was going to confront Mr. Fuck Face, but before I did, I sent a text to Ms. Customer Service Manager saying that the gig was up, and this message was from Myriah telling her to fuck right off.

I went back into the room where I slept with the man I thought was of my dreams and stood before him. I felt vulnerable and like I was naked on national television. I quietly called his name, but he did not stir, I then said it more loudly, but still, he did not budge. I then shook him until he woke. For some reason, I first apologized for stealing his phone and violating his privacy. And then I screamed, "what the actual fuck?!”. I admitted that I knew what he had been up to and proceeded to scream, "Lucy? Really? Amanda!!" (Ms. Customer Service and the Manager's wife).

Really? How dare you make me feel unstable when I had every reason to question what you have been up to.

I hurled the phone at him, and much to my surprise, he was very calm. Cooler than a cucumber, he took his phone back and asked me what I was talking about. I told him I had read everything. I saw everything and I needed to know it all. He dared to say I read or saw nothing, that there was nothing to see. He said all of this with such conviction that I started to wonder if I read too much into this and regretted not taking screenshots and texting them to myself. Was I an idiot? Myriah, shake it off! You can read English and comprehend everything you read. Then Luke's phone started going off. Text messages, phone calls. It was from Ms. Customer Service Manager. Yes, yes, yes, now everything is in the open. Caught! I knew from that moment my life would never be the same.

The hilarious thing was that Mr. Caught with Evidence was not having any of my ridiculous accusations. He thought it best we talk in the morning. I could not believe my ears. He calmly tucked his phone under his pillow and laid back down. I was going to explode! Avoidance at its finest. He didn't want to deal with my grief and silly stories so that was that. Conversation over. I left the room, took all the support I could get from my most loyal friend, my dog, and tried to figure out what I would do. My entire life was tied to this person. I had no savings or resources because everything I had was tied to this life - money, my heart, my dreams, my love, and my future. I had no self-esteem left, no confidence, no self-worth. My life seemed to be over!

The following day was business as usual. Luke got up to go to work as if nothing had happened and tried to avoid me like the plague. He just went through his routine, grabbed a Red Bull, and went on his merry way. I lay silently in the spare room bed like I was in a bunker in the middle of a war, thinking if I stayed so very still, nothing terrible would happen to me. What do I do? I felt that I was going to get into trouble for some reason. I was so conditioned to think that everything that happened was my fault. Somehow, I did this to us. I drove him to this! How and why did I feel this way?

I heard the side door shut, the garage door open, and off he went. Not a single word to be spoken.

I laugh thinking about this now, but what a great tactic. Avoidance is a great defense. The less he says or does, the more I wonder about what I saw or did not see, the more I was in my own head. Was I making this up because none of this seemed to affect him? I couldn't tell anyone because I was humiliated and had no evidence. Why didn't I take screenshots? As the blood rushed to my brain as I played detective last night, did I have another moment of insanity? I was now questioning myself again. Gosh, I was in hell!

In the meantime, we were two weeks away from another epic event planned for Mr. I Just Blew Up My Life, a turning forty party organized by his faithful partner. It was going to be a fabulous event, and the guests invited were so excited to attend another grand celebration at our expense. This time money and business had nothing to do with it. They knew this was going to be a spectacle. If Myriah was at the planning table and had a passion for making her man happy, then it would be good. I had so many great ideas and plans. Around our mini mansion was a half-acre of land, and the house sat in the middle of the most lavish lawn. With a panoramic view of the mountains, a party to end all parties was going to happen. Torches were going to surround the perimeter of the house. A DJ spinning lounge house vibes when you enter the house. Tray served prosecco and hors d'oeuvres for ease of guests to mingle and wish their beloved Luke a happy fortieth year of living on this earth.

The energy would ramp up as people arrive, they would hear great music and make themselves comfortable. There would be different drink stations (Luke loved to drink, and alcohol was an integral part of any gathering). There would be dancers (professional) as fun entertainment and then a tribute with an incredible cake for Mr. Not So Amazing. People talked about what they would wear, and many decided to stay at local hotels to partake in this epic event. But could I pull this off and pretend as if nothing had changed? I was brought up on emotional blackmail in a

European family. How could I possibly think about ruining this man's right to celebrate his fortieth birthday? How dare I even contemplate this. Not only would I let the birthday boy down, but I would also be letting down 60 of our guests and friends. But where did my feelings come into play? One thing I do know about me is that what you see is typically what you get. Could I celebrate this man and stay silent? Would I continue this charade when Mr. Nothing is Wrong, won't even talk to me about what I read the other night? He wouldn’t acknowledge it, verify it, deny it for that matter or have a civil conversation about it. I thought, no - I will not honour my generous offer to host and plan this party. So, I decided to cancel it.

Invites went out by an invitation program, and so I would cancel the invites via this same method. The event was two weeks out, and at this point, I didn't give a flying fuck what people thought. I knew I wasn't going to continue planning and ignore everything that happened. I opened my computer and then the program.

I pressed cancel on the invite without explanation and then let fate work its magic. Well, I counted down 3, 2, and 1 in my head, and my text message notifications started to go off, my home phone started ringing, and my cell phone started buzzing. People wanted to know what was wrong and if everything was okay. Lastly someone wrote: "Did you find out?". Wow! That last one stung. What did they mean? Did I know? Did people already know what Luke was up to? What a curious question. I ignored all my notifications and sent Luke a text to inform him that I canceled his party and would not continue this façade of a relationship when he didn't even have the decency to come clean with me. He didn't respond and again brushed it off like it was no big deal.

I felt an enormous pressure lifted from my heart. I took my first stance on this issue. I had the strength to make a statement. Whether Luke cared or not at this point did not matter to me. I took a small step to stick up for myself and not let him control every movement I made. I felt like I reclaimed at least an ounce of my power. I wanted Luke to admit his wrongdoings and how he hurt me. Going back to the first few months we were dating, all I asked for was mutual respect. I'm a big girl and an adult. My only rule was for Mr. Deflection to be honest, and if he found someone better or more compatible with him, he would clean his own house first and then move on. I felt it wasn't too much to ask. Apparently, it was too much, but now I have taken back some of my power. If Luke were to be honest and own up to his mistakes, if indeed they were mistakes, I'm so sure I would have been open to a conversation.

Have you fallen into another penis at inappropriate times? I sure have, so I know the draw of living in the moment and having a discretional affair. I'm no angel, and I can own my indiscretions. I can have a discussion, even if it’s not easy. Yet every time I tried to talk to Luke about my new revelations, he would say that I didn't see what I read on his cell phone and that I was crazy and paranoid. This made me insane.

Ask Yourself and Meaningful Journaling

This section is meant to reflect on your own story and thoughtfully reflect on your relationships.

____

____

____

Should we have access to each other's social media, smartphones, etc.?

____

____

____

Should our partners freely talk about any items that make us feel insecure?

____

____

____

Do you feel that you need to take your power back? If so, what is the one thing you can do today to regain your own power?

____

____

____

THE RANT FROM THE ROOM DOWN THE HALL

Things started to go downhill fast. I was trying to make a stance by "moving" into the spare bedroom. I would carry on with my day and then sleep in separate quarters. I would insist that my dog come into the room with me. I thought this would force Luke to confront the issue. When he got home and went to "our" room, he would hurl random hurtful comments down the hall that I was being ridiculous and that I didn't know anything. I would invite him to discuss, but the insults would come faster and more robustly. Imagine how ridiculous this would have sounded and looked to anyone witnessing this embarrassing juvenile behaviour. I would get sucked into the screaming conversation due to my frustration. I wanted him to love me, talk to me, and say I'm sorry. My hopeful anticipation of him apologizing or owning his actions caused me much frustration. I was hoping for some compassion for my hurt heart and the humiliation I was feeling. What would I tell my mother? What will I say to my friends? My life was my dream, being a stepmother was my heart's fulfillment, and loving Luke was everything I had worked towards. In reality, it was sort of crazy that I wanted him and his dysfunctional way of life, but I truly felt like I loved him and didn't want to live without him.

The following two weeks or so felt like a lifetime. I couldn't go on this way, but I didn't have any savings or way of moving on. I felt like a prisoner. My heart did not want to give up on this, my brain told me to run, and the reality was that I was stuck exactly in the middle. I was broken, and I was tired. But somehow, I still needed validation because Mr. I Will Never Own Up to My Wrongdoing would not concede to anything he was up to. So, I thought I would super sleuth it up one more time. I decided to check his voicemail. What are the chances he hadn't changed his passwords since I figured out his smartphone code? Nope, he didn't change anything. It was almost like he was so arrogant that he didn't think I would dig further. So, into voicemail I went, and low and behold, there was no mistake. Everything I read in the text messages was confirmed by personalized messages left on his voice recordings. Ms. Customer Service Manager was leaving messages about the trips they took while Luke was travelling for 'business.' I knew their every move, and so there it was. I had everything I needed to move on. I'm pissed off and perhaps more at myself than anyone else. How could I let this happen? Why did I not want to see this earlier? Why did I waste so many years of my life in this situation? I felt so ludicrous, and I'm far from stupid.

I have to take my next steps; the only way I can is to come clean with my friends and family. I started sharing my news with my friends, and not many people were surprised. Much to my shock, people were wondering if I would find out and when I was going to get the memo.

People shared that his shenanigans were so blatant that he didn't even hide them. Many people thought I knew and was okay with his philandering with women because he did not attempt to cover up his tracks while at bars and socializing. I felt like I could not have been more humiliated. I don't know what was worse, my broken heart or being humiliated beyond belief.

My mother was going to be heartbroken. She loved Mr. Spoiled My Mother Rotten, and I wasn't sure how she would take the news. Worse than that, we needed to tell the kids. We kept up a front and played house nicely when the kids were over because this was our drama, not theirs. I begged Mr. Daddy to let us tell them together. I would never rat out their dad, and he knew that. I loved those munchkins more than anything, and he knew that too, so I thought he would extend some grace my way so that we could explain the situation to them together. Nothing could have been further from the truth. When Luke brought them home at the end of the weekend, he told them in the car and guess who was not on that car ride. You guessed it. Me! How could he? Should I have been surprised that he reneged on his promise?

Over and over, the disappointment and letdown were chronic. Nothing surprised me at this point anymore.

Funnily enough though, Luke asked me not to tell my mother. Ha! That was a curious request, and for what reason, I still do not know to this day. I grabbed my cell phone and took my dog for a walk in order to call my mom and tell her all the news. I felt like I was going to faint as I dialed her number. She answered promptly, and she could tell something was wrong. I told her the condensed story, and she started questioning me as if I was for real or perhaps mistaken about what had happened, because there was no way Luke would treat me that way. It was like I had to convince my mom that all of this was happening to me. She dared to ask how Luke was doing with all of this. I felt like screaming, but, clearly, he had a hold on several of us. Why would I think I was the only victim of his cruel and insane ways?

I was ready to move on.

Ask Yourself and Meaningful Journaling

This section is meant to reflect on your own story and thoughtfully reflect on your relationships.

____

____

____

Do you feel alone in your relationship? What makes you feel that way?

____

____

____

I felt at times things would magically get better. Do you ever feel like things will get better without help or something changing? Identify what that might be.

____

____

____

THE PROPOSAL, I MEAN MOVING OUT

The countdown to the move was on. The closer it got; the scarcer Luke was. He was being his overgenerous self, allowing me to take whatever I needed. We still had the townhouse that Luke bought before we moved into his mini-mansion dream home. We had been trying to rent it out, but thankfully it was still vacant, and that is where I was to live. I started packing and was on my way just like that. There did not seem to be remorse or second thoughts except for the daily reminders that we would not be in this situation if I could just be rational about my thoughts toward Luke and his wrongdoings.

Until the bitter end, everything seemed to be my doing (that I did not do), so I had to succumb to the fact that everything was my fault. Moving forward, if that was going to set me free, then so be it. I just wanted to move on. The moving company was secured, and the first day of the rest of my life was scheduled. The night before the big move, Luke decided he was coming home. Late, albeit, but he crawled into our bed which I slept in because he wasn't home much in the last few weeks. It was as if I travelled back in time, and my sweet man had come home after a long day of work to get some rest and be with his girlfriend. I tried not to stir because I was not expecting this. Why was this happening? Was it adding insult to injury or just a sick joke? I loved this person. I wanted to wrap myself around him and feel his body next to mine, and I never wanted to let him go. How could I feel this way after all that had happened? The grief was so palpable that I couldn't breathe. I was drowning in sorrow. I was raw from having my life exposed, and I was more scared than I had ever been in my life. I tried to sleep, but the morning came so fast—the moment I had been dreading. I went to get up, and Luke was still in bed. He got up, turned around and put his arms around me. We cried together and held each other so very tightly. I couldn't bear it. I was sobbing as if I'd never cried before in my life. When people say that they know people who have died from a broken heart, I know how those people would have felt. Being stabbed to death would have been less painful. Luke went on to tell me what a fantastic person I was, not only to him, but to his children and family.

We were still hanging on to each other, and I felt I was at the altar in a fantastic romance novel with my knight in shining armour professing his love for me in front of our friends and family. I was dumbfounded by all the beautiful things he was telling me. Was this a mistake and a massive prank? Was this when Luke realized that he had made a big mistake and that we would call off the movers because it was all just a bad dream? Everything lovely you could ever want to hear from your man was coming from his lips, flittering into my eardrums. This was the moment, the time when he dropped to his knees and begged me to stay. But the façade stopped after some time; we wiped our tears, Luke got dressed and then he walked straight out the door. Just like that!

Still reeling from the sweet words of love and his gracious rendition of a romantic movie, I needed to start directing the movers to what was leaving the nest and to focus on the start of my new life. I was getting too old for this shit. How many times do I have to start my life over? But from a survival and sanity standpoint, this move had to happen. The moving truck door slammed shut, and my dog and I were off to start our new life on our own.

No more Luke, no more kids, alone and on my own.

As I moved back to our previous family home, I wondered if this was the best plan. So many memories were in this space and with an empty bedroom where the kids and dogs used to sleep. Where we entertained friends and family and where the lies and mental abuse continued and returned. I would try and make this better for me. A place to heal but still surrounded by the past, or perhaps hanging on to what I had—clinging to memories that were being swiftly ripped from me.

I paid the movers after they had loaded the last of the boxes into the basement. A few friends were coming to meet me to do the inaugural 'welcome back to your old new home and sorry for your devastating life.' I was looking forward to getting some support and love. As I was waiting, my phone rang. It was Luke. "Hello?" I said. Luke says, "Hey, I've been driving around all morning. I think I just made the biggest mistake of my life!" As stunned as I was to hear the admission, I think

I had just had enough for the day. I said, "what's done is done" and I hung up the phone.

Ask Yourself and Meaningful Journaling

This section is meant to reflect on your own story and thoughtfully reflect on your relationships.

____

____

____

How would you decide that enough is enough? What steps do you need to take to move forward?

____

____

____

SUICIDE

I felt like my entire life was stripped of me. How did I get here? One day I'm in love with my man, loving his young sons and dreaming of the coming days. Now, I live in a place by myself. I'm exhausted from trying to work out why people who love each other would oppress each other. Before I met Luke, I took a certificate course for Life Coaching before life coaching became a popular term. Even though this teaching does not make you a therapist, I felt so bad that I decided to implement my previous learnings. I started my 'should list' every day. I should not feel this bad, I should fix the fridge handle, I should move on, and I should never see Luke again. But I set myself up for failure because I was doing none of these things. I was like an addict. I was looking for a way to keep seeing Luke, and because I still worked for his business, I had every opportunity to do so. But grief is so taxing on your body. I would try to live each day through the motions of trying to work, staying uplifted, and looking for the positive or learning opportunity from this situation. I couldn't find any explanation for why I deserved this type of pain in my life. I tried to numb myself with excessive drinking because, for a moment, I could relax and let my pain drown in wine. Nighttime was the worst. I could not sleep, cried for days, and became a skeleton of the woman I think I once was ten years before. I was a career woman with dreams of perhaps having a baby with a partner I could love the rest of my life. I replayed the whys, what ifs, and how could this happen to me?

Simply put, I felt overall I was an excellent human and believed in the universe and karma. So how was this happening to me? I felt I was the only person in the world that had gone through something so heinous. I was tortured for years, feeling like I was not good enough, that I was always trying to measure up to some imaginary standard and prove myself to others. I had been a slave to this man's whims and deceptive actions and behaviour. I wondered how I brought all of this to my life. I felt weak and didn't know how I could ever trust myself with men again. These thoughts kept my brain whirling, and I tried to find any kind of explanation to make sense of it all. I had never heard of the term narcissism, or any terms related to that disorder. I could only tell myself that somehow, I had brought this upon myself and deserved this type of treatment. I was spinning out of control because I was pretending to be fine when I was not. I tried to hold it together when I could no longer do so. I needed the pain to end. I needed the negative talk to end and to find myself again, a capable woman who always saw the bright side of everyone, of everything, and of life.

I was out one night and pathetically recounted everything that happened over dinner with a friend. It was like I was living outside my body, not believing that I was going through this.

I was driving home, and it was raining. I was crying because I felt helpless. I was exhausted, and I could not take the pain anymore. I felt alone and pathetic. I got home and pressed the garage door opener. I drove my truck into the garage and closed the door. I felt at that moment that if I could go to sleep and not wake up, I would be in a better place than I currently was. I rolled down my driver-side window. As the garage door shut, I wondered how long it would take to be at rest. I tried to calculate in my head how long this method would take, even though I did not know anything about it. I just needed the pain to stop, the humiliation to end, the exhausting justifications to cease, and mostly never wanting to be in this situation again.

I leaned into the idea that I could expire this way. I started to think about what I still had in my life and what I had left. Sadly, the only thing I could think of was my dog. I loved my dog so much. No matter what was going on, Sergeant was there for me. For years, when I was lonely or left feeling worthless, he knew I needed love. When I felt like I was going crazy and questioned my sanity, he always sat by my side. My dog Sergeant was my only ride or die at that moment. Who was going to love him if I decided to end my life? He did not deserve the same type of treatment that I was served, and why would I treat him the same? I loved him and couldn't leave him. I owed him a lifetime of love in return for him loving me. I promptly turned off the engine and opened the garage door. I walked into the house, collapsed to the floor, and my loyal friend ran to the door to greet me with all the love and respect he always extended and, frankly, what I deserved. I sat on the floor for a long time and just cried, pet my best friend, and promised I would get some help. I decided to go to bed and believed there would be better days ahead.

As I had committed to doing, I went to see my physician the next day and was lucky she had a spot open to see me. I've been with my doctor for several years, and we had a good rapport. When my doctor entered the exam room, she looked at me with concern as though she didn't recognize me.

She then logged into her computer and checked my records. She asked how she could assist, and I blurted out that I needed help and needed it now. I omitted the garage incident from the night before. She took the time to hear my story with enough compassion for someone who is her patient but a personal friend. She understood that I was exhausted and not getting the rest or relief from the grief that I so desperately needed. She admitted she did not recognize the patient she had been treating for years and knew I needed immediate help. We discussed starting with antidepressants and getting some crucial assistance. She also asked me to see a counsellor immediately and led me to a website where I could find a therapist that could relate best to me. I needed this direction. I needed someone to hold my hand to lead me to get the help that I so needed. I felt relief that someone that didn't know me intimately could recognize and see my pain. See what was happening to me emotionally and physically. I desperately wanted to be seen and heard, and she understood intrinsically. She understood that I needed help but that I also needed to help myself.

Talk Suicide Canada

If you or someone you know is thinking about suicide, call Talk Suicide Canada at 1-833-456-4566 (24/7) or text 45645 (4 PM - 12 AM ET).

For residents of Québec, call 1 866 APPELLE (1-866-277-3553) (24/7) or visit suicide.ca.

Ask Yourself and Meaningful Journaling

This section is meant to reflect on your own story and thoughtfully reflect on your relationships.

____

____

____

TEN YEARS LATER

Medication was an excellent short-term treatment for my situation. My emotions could level off so that I could stop feeling like I was reeling out of control. I was given a limited number of sleeping pills to learn how to sleep again, which alleviated my exhaustion. And it helped immensely to consult with someone who didn't know me, could objectively listen to me, and authentically extract my feelings so that I could examine how best to move forward. My therapist worked with me to decide on how to move forward in my life. She half-joked that it might be a clever idea for her to pay me to visit because she wasn't sure what type of ridiculous situation would be shared with her weekly. I guess that's the thing about living with a narcissist and losing everything you once thought about yourself and the strength you brought to this world. I believe that is why so many people that live through this type of abuse don't share their experiences because it's too crazy even to fathom and likely would not be believed—wondering what people would think if you told them your stories. They would wonder why you wouldn't just walk away. Why you wouldn't just say to the perpetrator to go fuck themselves and not allow them to treat you in such a manner. There is a bizarre sense of control that a narcissist has over you, and it's like an addiction. You are tied to this person, and you can't leave, you can't defend yourself, and you feel entirely helpless. You keep getting pulled into a whirlwind of lies, humiliation, and nonsensical rhetoric. You just stay.

I can say today that I was essentially useless for the first three years after the tragic day I wanted to end it all. I worked hard to try and trust myself again, to regain the knowledge that I was not crazy and illogical. I tried to find the woman I once was who was filled with gratitude and positive energy, who had a can and will do attitude. I needed to find that person again in myself.

Like an addict, I fell off the Luke wagon a few times and would fall into bed, and at one point entered a weird imaginary stage where I thought we could be friends or that he would change. But every time I made that mistake, I came out of it knowing that he was toxic and would never change. Thankfully, the boys' mother was gracious enough to allow me to see the kids twice a month. This was a generous gift; she knew that I had only good intentions when it came to her sons and that I absolutely loved them. These acts of kindness helped me so very much. I started to believe in people again and that I would recover. A few times in my life, I have been compared to a pit bull, and I took this as an insult at the time. However, the pit bull in me was there, was tough, and wanted to survive, and live. I wanted to prove to myself that I was strong and capable and that I could rebuild my life.

I found love again in my work, which was unrelated to manufacturing and outside of the industry that I got so tangled in. I purposefully separated myself from any toxicity in people and situations. I started working for a non-profit and enjoyed my financial autonomy again. I would be lying if I didn't admit that Luke did help me financially while I was trying to recover. Whether it was because of generosity or guilt over bringing me to my knees, assistance was welcomed and needed. This help allowed me time to mend and rebuild.

After I decided to move out of the house that reminded me of the life I once had, the real healing began. I sold all the expensive guilt gifts Luke had bought me and cleaned house. Not only physically but in the attic of my mind that held on to these things. Every day became a step toward the person I once was, but stronger.

I went on to excel in my job at the non-profit and started winning awards. Each time I was recognized, I knew that the work I put back into myself was paying off, and people saw it.

When I reflect on those years, I realize that, without them, I would not be the person that I am today. However, this was a hard lesson, and I would not want anyone to suffer in this manner. While sharing my story with other people, it has come to my attention that so many people suffer living with a narcissist. Not diminishing my situation, but I have heard horror stories about not only mental abuse but physical abuse as well. Whenever we share this story and our dream of authoring a book like this, people immediately open up. We first see a flicker of people recognizing this pain and then readily sharing accounts of their own similar experiences. If this story helps people say that I, too, lived this or are currently living this, then we feel that reliving years of mental abuse and sharing this book is worth it tenfold.

This book is meant to be a share and reflect story of sorts with self-introspection and perhaps acknowledgment that you too could be in this situation. Our hope is it will help others recognize similar narcissistic behaviours and then journal about these experiences. The more self-realized we are in these situations, the better. Writing about my experience has been cathartic for me. As exhausting as this revisiting of my life has been, it has helped tremendously in my healing. To be very transparent, I am still not convinced that even after ten years of recovery, I am able to have a healthy relationship again. Still, I continue working towards finding a loving and trusting relationship because I deserve it! And so do each one of you.

Ask Yourself and Meaningful Journaling

This section is meant to reflect on your own story and thoughtfully reflect on your relationships.

____

____

____

If you decide that you need to move forward, what steps are required to do so?

____

____

____

What fuels your future passions so that you can take the steps needed to break free?

____

____

____

What empowers you and will build back your confidence?

____

____

____

Self-love is important for healing. What are the things that you love about yourself?

____

____

____

REFERENCES

Baskin-Sommers, A., Krusemark, E., & Ronningstam, E. (2014). Empathy in narcissistic personality disorder: from clinical and empirical perspectives. Personality Disorders: Theory, Research, and Treatment, 5(3), 323.

Day, N. J. (2021). The impact of narcissistic personality disorder on others: A study of romantic partners and family members.

Kjærvik, S. L., & Bushman, B. J. (2021). The link between narcissism and aggression: A meta-analytic review. Psychological Bulletin, 147(5), 477.

Levy, K. N. (2012). Subtypes, dimensions, levels, and mental states in narcissism and narcissistic personality disorder. Journal of clinical psychology, 68(8), 886-897.

Sparks , D. (2020, September 15). Narcissistic personality disorder: Inflated sense of importance. Retrieved January 8, 2023, from https://newsnetwork.mayoclinic.org/discussion/narcissistic-personality-disorder-inflated-sense-of-importance/

Stark, C. A. (2019). Gaslighting, misogyny, and psychological oppression. The monist, 102(2), 221-235.

Songwriters: Green Dallas John

Save Your Scissors lyrics © Emi April Music Inc., Bald Headed Boys Inc.

ABOUT THE AUTHOR

Maria's work is about being mindful, motivated, and memorable. A place where we can be inspired by others, therefore, inspiring ourselves.

Maria Maria Binder is the 2018 Recipient of the MPI Award of Excellence and the 2018 Recipient of the Women of Inspiration Innovative Leader Award.

By sharing our personal stories and journeys, we are open to discussions and creating a safe environment for us to connect and grow. Stronger together. Let's learn from one another and create a world that is more accepting of helping each other by supporting and showing empathy for every person.

Manufactured by Amazon.ca
Bolton, ON

32054067R00096